6489

DATE DUE

Metro Litho
Oak Forest, IL 60452

SEP 2 9 1997			
NOV 1 2 1998			

AMERICA the BEAUTIFUL

VIRGINIA

By Sylvia McNair

Consultants

Edward D. C. Campbell, Jr., Ph.D., Editor, *Virginia Cavalcade*, Virginia State Library and Archives, Richmond

Seymour B. Stiss, Supervisor of Social Studies, Arlington Public Schools

Helen Coalter, Department Chairman, Social Studies, Franklin Military School, Richmond; Assistant State Coordinator, Virginia Bicentennial of the Constitution Competition

Robert L. Hillerich, Ph.D., Bowling Green State University, Bowling Green, Ohio

CHILDRENS PRESS ®

CHICAGO

Two young boys fishing in the Shenandoah River

Project Editor: Joan Downing
Associate Editor: Shari Joffe
Design Director: Margrit Fiddle
Typesetting: Graphic Connections, Inc.
Engraving: Liberty Photoengraving

Library of Congress Cataloging-in-Publication Data

McNair, Sylvia.
    America the beautiful. Virginia / by Sylvia McNair.
        p.   cm.
    Includes index.
    Summary: Introduces the geography, history,
government, economy, culture, famous people, and
historic sites of the Old Dominion.
    ISBN 0-516-00492-1
    1. Virginia—Juvenile literature.
[1. Virginia] I. Title.
F226.3.M63 1989
975.5—dc19   88-38203
                                                      CIP
                                                      AC

St. John's Church, in Richmond, where Patrick Henry gave his famous "Give Me Liberty or Give Me Death!" speech

TABLE OF CONTENTS

Chapter 1

THE OLD DOMINION

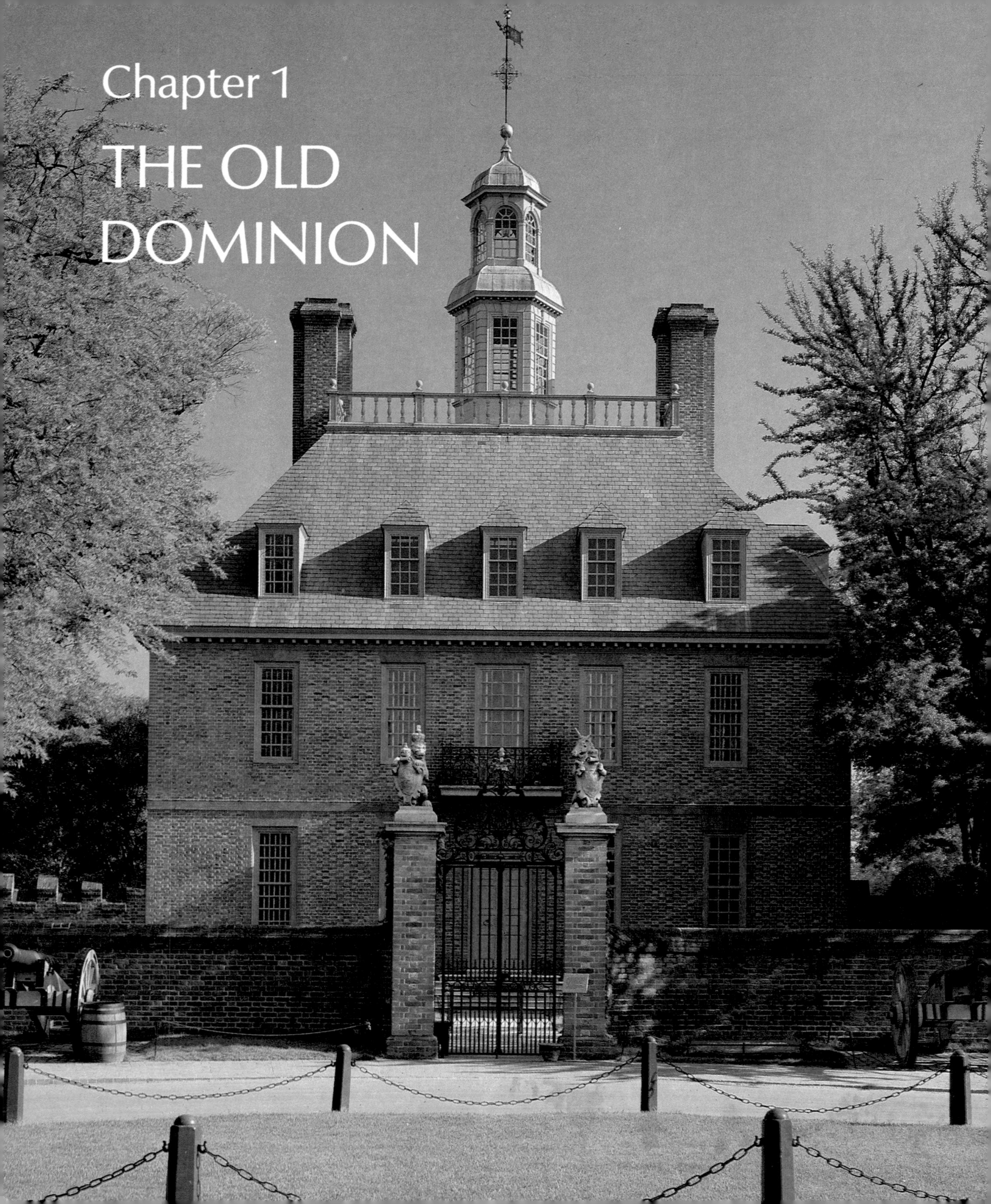

THE OLD DOMINION

May 14, 1607. This was the day, nearly four hundred years ago, when the first permanent English settlement in what is now the United States was established on Jamestown Island.

These Englishmen were not the first people who lived in this country. Native Americans had roamed the beautiful hills and valleys for thousands of years before them. They were not even the first European settlers; Spanish adventurers and missionaries were already exploring Florida and the Southwest.

But in a very real sense, these few adventurous men who came to Jamestown were fathers of the nation. They established the Virginia Colony, a colony called the Old Dominion by King Charles II of England. This was the first of thirteen colonies that together would rebel against England 170 years later and form the United States of America. Eight states eventually were carved from the Virginia Colony's land.

Virginia offers variety and wonderment at every turn. Ocean shore, peaceful bays, grand valleys, rugged mountains, teeming cities, and sleepy hamlets—all are Virginia. But above all, the family heritage of Virginians throughout the state brings to them a personal and intimate familiarity with history. Virginia is a symbol of endurance, pride, and freedom. It is the Old Dominion, Mother of Presidents, Mother of States.

Chapter 2

THE LAND

THE LAND

Equal to the promised land in fertility,
and far superior to it for beauty.
—Washington Irving's description of western Virginia

The mainland of Virginia is shaped roughly like a triangle. On the west, Virginia is bordered by Kentucky, and on the northwest, by West Virginia. Except for the area of Washington, D.C., which dips into the state, most of Virginia's northeast border is formed by the Potomac River, which is shared with Maryland. On the east, the state is bounded by Chesapeake Bay and the Atlantic Ocean. The straight southern boundary is shared with North Carolina and Tennessee. A small part of Virginia is not connected by land to the rest of the state. It is called the Eastern Shore, and it is part of a peninsula reaching down from Maryland between Chesapeake Bay and the Atlantic Ocean.

TOPOGRAPHY

Virginia is thirty-sixth in total area among the fifty states. It covers 40,767 square miles (105,586 square kilometers); this includes 1,063 square miles (2,753 square kilometers) of inland water. The northern tip of the state is 200 miles (322 kilometers) from its southern border. The western corner is 440 miles (708 kilometers) from the Atlantic coastline, and is farther west than Detroit, Michigan. In altitude, the land rises from sea level at the

The Great Falls of the Potomac River

coast to more than a mile high in the mountains of southwestern Virginia. The highest point in Virginia is Mount Rogers, 5,729 feet (1,746 meters) above sea level. The land can be divided into three regions: the Tidewater, or Coastal Plain; the Piedmont, in the central portion of the state; and the Mountain and Valley Region in the western reaches of the state.

THE TIDEWATER

The first settlements in Virginia were established along the coast, in the Coastal Plain. This region is also known as Tidewater Virginia, or simply the Tidewater, because the ocean's tides enter Chesapeake Bay and the wide mouths of the region's four rivers— the Potomac, Rappahannock, York, and James.

Wild Chincoteague ponies make their home on Assateague Island, which is part of Virginia's Eastern Shore.

The waters of Chesapeake Bay and the four rivers divide the Tidewater, geographically, into four parts. The Eastern Shore is a peninsula, 70 miles (113 kilometers) long, that is cut off from the mainland of Virginia by Chesapeake Bay. By land, it can be reached from the state of Maryland, to the north, or by the Chesapeake Bay Bridge-Tunnel from the city of Virginia Beach, to the south. Much of the Eastern Shore is secluded, a home for wild ponies and large flocks of snow geese. There are wide beaches, lagoons, and tiny offshore islands.

Along the mainland, three long, narrow peninsulas reach out like fingers into the bay: one between the Potomac and the Rappahannock rivers, the second between the Rappahannock and the York, and the third between the York and the James.

At the mouth of the James River is a deep harbor called Hampton Roads. The cities of Newport News, Hampton, Portsmouth, and Norfolk front on Hampton Roads.

The level, sandy land of the Tidewater is easily cultivated. Large plantations once occupied much of the area, producing abundant

Blue grosbeaks (above), hummingbirds (top right), and orioles (bottom right) are among the hundreds of birds common to the Great Dismal Swamp region.

crops. The waters of Chesapeake Bay are famous for the quantity and quality of their fish and shellfish.

In the southeast corner of the state, south of Hampton Roads and the bustling seaport cities that surround it, is a beautiful area with an unfortunate name, the Great Dismal Swamp. George Washington called the 63,000-acre (25,495-hectare) region "a glorious paradise." It is a wildlife refuge, alive with birds and animals. Rare species of birds are often spotted here, and more than a hundred kinds are classified as common to the region. Among the latter are such colorful varieties as orioles, scarlet tanagers, blue grosbeaks, and ruby-throated hummingbirds. Some seventeen kinds of warblers fill the air with their songs.

THE PIEDMONT

West of the Tidewater is a region called the Piedmont. The Piedmont gets its name from the French words meaning "foot of the mountain." This central region of the state has rolling countryside—gentle hills and fertile river valleys that mark the change from the Coastal Plain. The hills become higher and steeper toward the west.

The Piedmont is wedge-shaped, about 40 miles (64 kilometers) wide in the north of the state and about 185 miles (298 kilometers) from east to west along the southern border. The Piedmont and the Tidewater regions are separated by a "fall line." This is where the rivers flowing toward the Atlantic Ocean fall from a hard rock bed to a softer rock bed on the plain below. The cities of Alexandria, Fredericksburg, Richmond, Petersburg, and Emporia were built along the fall line.

The part of the Piedmont south of the James River, known as Southside Virginia, is planted largely in tobacco and peanuts. Livestock, grains, cotton, and dairy products are the principal products of the rest of the Piedmont.

The hills, woods, and numerous artificially created lakes of the Piedmont area provide attractive areas for camping, fishing, and other recreational activities.

MOUNTAINS AND VALLEYS

To the west of the Piedmont, in western Virginia, the hills give way to the Blue Ridge Mountains. The Blue Ridge marches from the northern tip of the state—only a few miles west of Washington, D.C.—in a southwesterly direction through the state and into North Carolina.

Shenandoah National Park, in the Blue Ridge Mountains of Virginia, contains such spectacular scenery as rock formations called natural chimneys and beautiful, cascading waterfalls.

Shenandoah National Park, one of the loveliest areas in the United States, is located in the Blue Ridge. It contains awe-inspiring rock formations—natural columns, "chimneys," and bridges. But the park includes only a small portion of the natural wonders of western Virginia.

Numerous large and colorful limestone caverns lie beneath the mountains. In some places, beautiful waterfalls cascade over cliffs; in others, hot mineral springs bubble up from far below the land surface. Tourist resorts and spas in the vicinity of the springs have attracted visitors since before the American Revolution.

Mount Rogers, the highest point in the state, overlooks the southern end of the Blue Ridge.

West of and parallel to the Blue Ridge is the Great Appalachian Valley. Actually, the Great Valley of Virginia is made up of several valleys. The Shenandoah Valley, drained by the Shenandoah River, extends from the Maryland-Virginia line to

Buchanan County. *Shenandoah* is the name the Indians gave to the area; it means "daughter of the stars." The river and the valley around it are truly deserving of the name. These are stretches of broad, green bottomlands, where the land is productive and the views of the mountains are inspiring. Other major valleys in the region include the Fincastle Valley, between Buchanan and Christianburg; the Dublin Valley, between Christianburg and Marion; and the Abingdon Valley, between Marion and the Tennessee line.

The very edge of western Virginia, in the southwestern triangle between Tennessee and Kentucky, is part of the Appalachian Plateau. This area has mountains that range from about 2,000 to 3,000 feet (about 600 to 900 meters) in elevation. This is where the state's major coalfields lie. One of this area's landmarks is the Cumberland Gap—a gap or space in the Appalachian Mountains. Thousands upon thousands of pioneers traveled through this gap on their way westward. Rather than travel directly over the mountains, many traveled south to reach the gap and then traveled north again on the far side of the mountains.

CLIMATE

Virginia's climate varies from one part of the state to another. On the coast, the weather is mild and humid. Even in January, snowfall is light and afternoon temperatures are usually pleasantly cool, rather than cold. In January, the average temperature in the Coastal Plain is 41 degrees Fahrenheit (5 degrees Celsius); the snowfall is 5 to 10 inches (13 to 25 centimeters).

As the land rises toward the west, temperatures drop. Winters in the mountains can be quite severe. Snowstorms and ice storms

Thousands of pioneers, traveling westward along Daniel Boone's Wilderness Trail, cut through the Cumberland Gap, this break in the Appalachian Mountains.

heavy enough to cause the closing of mountain highways are not uncommon. The average January temperature in the mountain regions is 32 degrees Fahrenheit (0 degrees Celsius), and snowfall is about 25 to 30 inches (64 to 76 centimeters).

Summers in the mountains are refreshing and pleasant, with temperatures averaging several degrees below that on the valley floors. In July, coastal temperatures average 78 degrees Fahrenheit (26 degrees Celsius); the mountain region's average is 68 degrees Fahrenheit (20 degrees Celsius).

Northwest Virginia receives about 36 inches (91 centimeters) of precipitation, including rain, melted snow, and other moisture. In the southern areas of the state, precipitation is about 44 inches (112 centimeters).

Variations in climate have an important effect on farmers' growing seasons. There are about 240 frost-free days at the coast, but only 150 in the mountainous west. This means that coastal Virginia has a growing season that is more than eight months long—three months longer than that of western Virginia.

Chapter 3
THE PEOPLE

THE PEOPLE

From the beginning, most of Virginia's population has been of Anglo-Saxon stock. Virginia did not experience the wave of immigrants who came to the industrial cities of the North in the late 1800s and early 1900s. This means that many of today's Virginians can trace their roots back through several generations of Virginians.

RELIGION

The first settlers of the Virginia Colony were members of the Anglican (Episcopal) Church. They were followed, during the Colonial period, by German Lutherans, Welsh Baptists, and English Quakers.

The Anglican Church was the established church of the Virginia Colony. In 1786, a law establishing religious toleration was passed by the general assembly. Thomas Jefferson was the author of the Virginia Statute of Religious Freedom, and he considered it to be one of his finest achievements.

Today, the majority of Virginians are Protestant Christians. The largest Protestant denominations are Baptist and Methodist. Roman Catholics and Jews are the next two largest religious groups.

POPULATION GROWTH

Virginia was the most populous of the original thirteen colonies. The first women arrived in 1619, and families were started. By 1700, the small band that survived those first rigorous winters had grown to a population of 70,000, 9 percent of whom were slaves. By 1715, the black population was about 25 percent, and in 1750, it had risen to 40 percent. In 1800, the colony had a population of more than 800,000, and by 1890, that figure had more than doubled.

The unfavorable economic conditions of the early 1900s sent many Virginians, black and white, to other states seeking employment. This trend was reversed when Virginia received a number of federal projects during the Great Depression of the 1930s.

In the last few decades, Virginia's population growth has exceeded that of the nation. Today, much of eastern Virginia is considered part of the great urban corridor along the East Coast.

POPULATION DISTRIBUTION

Until the early 1900s, Virginia's population was scattered throughout the state. At the beginning of the twentieth century, the population was 15 percent urban and 85 percent rural. Today, the population is primarily urban. Of every ten people in Virginia, seven live in a large metropolitan area, one lives in a small city, and two live in a rural community. Less than 20 percent of Virginians are nonwhite and less than 4 percent are foreign-born.

About a third of the three million people living in the Washington, D.C. metropolitan area live in Virginia. Another million or so Virginians live in the Norfolk-Virginia Beach-

Two of the most heavily populated regions of Virginia are the Washington, D.C. metropolitan area, which includes Alexandria (left), and the Norfolk-Newport News-Virginia Beach area (above).

Newport News area. Other major metropolitan areas include Richmond-Petersburg, Roanoke, Lynchburg, Charlottesville, Danville, and Bristol.

The geographic regions of Virginia have led to different lifestyles. Though these regional differences have been a source of pride, all Virginians recognize that to be born a Virginian is a special badge of honor. Virginians throughout the state share a reverence for the past and an abiding love for the Old Dominion.

Chapter 4
THE GROWTH OF A COLONY

THE GROWTH OF A COLONY

The first settlers arrived in the Virginia region more than five thousand years ago. Like the Indian settlers throughout North America, they were descendants of the peoples who had crossed the land bridge between Asia and America more than thirteen thousand years ago. These Indian settlers had traveled southward from the northern woodland areas. Originally, they were probably nomadic hunters who traveled and camped in small bands.

After a time, these Indians began to supplement their diet by gathering fruits, berries, nuts, and seeds. About seven or eight thousand years ago, they began to cultivate some crops—squash, beans, and maize (corn). As cultivation increased, the Indians found it more efficient to live in permanent dwellings and form larger communities. Living in communities led to the formation of social organizations.

THE POWHATAN

In the late 1500s and early 1600s, the tribes in the region of Virginia spoke dialects of the Algonquian language. They lived in houses made with saplings that were lashed together and covered with bark. Most of their settlements consisted of about fifty dwellings that were usually located near rivers. These Woodland Indians lived on game, fish, corn, beans, nuts, and berries. They also cultivated tobacco. They had tools with which they cleared

The lodges shown in artist John White's 1585 watercolor of an Indian village near Roanoke Island (right) are very much like those of the Powhatan Indians. A Powhatan lodge has been re-created at Jamestown Festival Park (above).

land, built houses, farmed, built canoes, and made clothing, baskets, and other personal belongings. Among the notable ornaments these Indians made were white or purple cylindrical beads worked from marine shells. These beads, called *wampum*, were treasured.

In the region that was to become Virginia, there was a loose confederation of about thirty Indian groups called the Powhatan. Among the groups in the alliance were the Pamunkey, Potomac, Rappahannock, and Chickahominy. The chief of the Powhatan Confederacy was Wahunsonacock, who later came to be known as simply Powhatan.

This picturesque and detailed map of Virginia was made by Captain John Smith.

THE VIRGINIA COLONY

During the 1500s, North America was visited by several waves of European adventurers, explorers, and missionaries. Many of these Europeans came to America, completed their explorations, and then returned home. Even those who made many journeys to the New World still considered Europe their home. It was not so for the small band of men who arrived at Jamestown in 1607.

Just imagine what it was like for those first few men who came to Jamestown in 1607. They had spent nearly five months on board three tiny ships, the *Susan Constant*, the *Godspeed*, and the *Discovery*. Nearly one-third of the original 144 who had sailed from England had died at sea.

Finally, a little piece of land appeared, in the mouth of a wide river. Jamestown Island—they named it for their king—must have looked like paradise after those many weeks at sea.

Many Jamestown buildings have been reconstructed at Jamestown Festival Park, not far from the site of the original settlement.

The Jamestown colonists had several goals. The king of England had granted a land charter to the Virginia Company of London on the condition that the company explore the area, build a fort, prepare for a larger settlement, and convert the native population to Christianity. All of the objectives rested on a single goal: economic gain. The colonists, and the investors who financed the venture, hoped that settlement of the Virginia Colony would lead to wealth for all. Perhaps Virginia would provide a product to sell in England and Europe; perhaps the explorations would lead to a shorter route to the East; perhaps the vastness of the Virginia Colony would create more wealth for England and weaken the New World claims of Spain and France.

In Jamestown, however, the colonists faced hardships far beyond those they had suffered at sea. They were remarkably ill-prepared for their undertaking. Few provisions had been brought from England. The colonists knew little of how to grow crops or hunt game. They had brought few tools with which to build shelter. Weakened from the long sea voyage and a poor diet, they

26

were subject to diseases. By the end of the first year, fewer than one-third of the original band survived.

The investors who had supplied the funds for the colony knew nothing of the extreme hardships faced by the colonists. Safe in England, they were optimistic about making fortunes from these new lands beyond the seas. They continued to recruit colonists to join the men already in Virginia.

In 1610, the fewer than sixty surviving colonists were so disheartened that they decided to give up and sail back home. But as they reached Hampton Roads, two ships approached—ships loaded with supplies and new colonists. They turned back, to try again.

The Virginia Company charter was rewritten twice, and as of 1612, the boundaries of the Virginia Colony included a vast area that today covers forty-two of the fifty states, part of southern Canada, and the island of Bermuda. The charter remained in effect until 1624. During that time, 7,289 immigrants came to Jamestown; 6,040 died, most of famine but others of disease, fevers, and war.

INDIAN RELATIONS

The Jamestown settlers, encroaching on the Powhatan Confederacy lands, were subject to the risk of Indian attacks. Throughout the early years, isolated skirmishes occurred both near the settlement and along the frontier. It was during one of these encounters that Captain John Smith was captured and later released. The story that he was saved by Pocahontas, Powhatan's daughter, is highly suspect. It is certain, however, that Pocahontas did have a role in the colony's development. In 1613, the English kidnapped the princess from her tribe. The leaders of the colony hoped that with Pocahontas as a hostage, they could bargain for the colony's safety from Indian attacks. Later that same year, colonist John Rolfe and Pocahontas fell in love. Their marriage in 1614 furthered the hope that relations between the settlement and the Indians would be strengthened. The couple sailed for England in 1616, hoping to raise money to help the Virginia colonists. Pocahontas died in 1618, on the eve of her scheduled return to Virginia.

The fragile peace between the Indians and the colonists was broken in 1622. Chief Powhatan had died, and the new chief of the Powhatan Confederacy decided to retaliate against the colonists, who had settled on Powhatan land. The first attack, in which 350 settlers were killed, began a long series of battles between the Indians and the colonists. Because the colonists had superior weapons, they were able to push the Indians farther and farther west. Finally, the Indians were forced entirely out of the peninsula between the James and York rivers and into lands west of the fall line.

TOBACCO RULES

During the times of relative peace at Jamestown, the Indians showed the settlers how to cultivate beans, squash, and corn. They taught the English how to hunt deer and wild turkey, and how to catch fish in weirs, or traps. If the colonists had heeded the Indians and planted crops, they might have been able to avoid the terrible starvation conditions of 1608-1610. But they did not. Instead, they turned their attention and energy to another crop introduced by the Indians—tobacco.

In 1612, John Rolfe experimented with the native tobacco crop and tobacco seeds from Trinidad. He developed a method for

Tobacco was a money-making industry for Virginia by 1628, when more than 500,000 pounds were shipped from Jamestown to Europe.

curing the leaves, and in 1614, he shipped the dried tobacco leaves to Europe. Smoking rapidly became a popular fashion in European society. The colony had, at last, found the product sought by the Virginia Company. Tobacco promised to make the company, the investors, and the planters wealthy. Rolfe shipped four barrels in 1614. Two years later, 2,500 pounds were shipped. The numbers grew: more than 18,000 pounds were shipped in 1617; 50,000 in 1618; and more than 500,000 pounds in 1628.

But tobacco had its share of critics. It was called "that chopping herbe of Hell," and "noxious weed." This was not without cause. Tobacco was a lucrative cash crop and planters favored it. Tobacco was planted while crops such as corn—needed to feed the colonists—were neglected. Tobacco was planted year after year, and within half a dozen years, the soil became exhausted.

Some tobacco farms, too large to be worked by the planter alone, were worked by indentured servants. Indentured servants

After the first women arrived in Jamestown in 1619, families were established and the colony grew.

were required to work for a master, either to satisfy a debt or in payment of a minor crime. Most of these servants were from England and Ireland, but in 1619 the first Africans were brought to Virginia to work as indentured servants. Blacks who were brought to Virginia before 1649 were not slaves.

Also in 1619, the first women arrived at the colony. The ninety women were "mail order brides"; the settlers who married them paid for the women's passage a price of 120 pounds of tobacco apiece.

In 1619, the colonists held elections. They chose members of a House of Burgesses, the first representative assembly in the New World. Now called the Virginia General Assembly, it is the oldest legislative body in the Western Hemisphere. The burgesses did not hold all the government power, however. They shared authority with a council chosen by the Virginia Company.

In 1624, King James I revoked the charter of the Virginia Company, and Virginia became a royal colony. The crown

The House of Burgesses, the first assembly in the New World made up of elected representatives, met for the first time in July 1619.

appointed royal governors — some of whom never set foot in Virginia — to serve as executive heads of the government.

BACON'S REBELLION

One of these governors was Sir William Berkeley, who served from 1642 to 1652 and again from 1660 to 1667. During his first term, Berkeley enjoyed good relations with the colonists. During his second term, however, Berkeley met strong opposition.

By the 1660s, some of the early colonists had become wealthy. They owned large tracts of good farmland along the coastal rivers. They had their own docks. Ships from London sailed right up to the wharves to pick up tobacco. The Tidewater plantations were self-contained communities; their many tenants, indentured servants, and slaves worked the land, practiced a variety of essential crafts, and turned a tidy profit for the landowners.

Meanwhile, life was different in the land away from the Tidewater. The frontier farmlands were less productive than those of the Tidewater; the farms were smaller and more difficult to work. The farmers raised tobacco, but the restrictive trade laws had pushed the price of the crop down. Furthermore, the frontier farmers needed protection from the Indians.

Governor Berkeley seemed unaware of the frontier's needs. He continued to favor the Tidewater region and its aristocracy. In 1674, the western farmers, led by Nathaniel Bacon, revolted against the royal governor.

Bacon's Rebellion led to the removal of Berkeley as governor of Virginia. In addition, certain legal rights were granted to the colony's citizens. Although some rights were won from the crown, many Virginians were dissatisfied. They felt that they had the right to govern themselves and to determine for themselves what taxes and tariffs were appropriate. This attitude existed throughout the colonies, but was exceptionally strong in Virginia.

COLONIAL WILLIAMSBURG

For almost a hundred years, Jamestown served as the seat of government for the Virginia Colony. It was a swampy, bug-infested village, not at all a pleasant place to do business. Its ramshackle buildings were often destroyed by fire, and in 1698 the statehouse burned for the fourth time.

The royal governor, Francis Nicholas, decided it was time to find a new site for the capital. After considering several different places, the House of Burgesses chose a location five miles (eight kilometers) upriver from Jamestown, a place called Middle Plantation. The small settlement there already had both a church (Bruton Parish Church) and a college (the College of William and Mary). Middle Plantation's name was later changed to Williamsburg, a name it has had ever since.

Costumed artisans and innkeepers give the reconstructed colonial capital of Williamsburg an aura of living history.
Among the sights to be seen are the capitol building (top left), a residential street (left), and a wheelwright shop (above).

Williamsburg's early city fathers had a vision. They wanted to build a great city like those of Europe, a center of religion and education as well as of government. The College of William and Mary, chartered in 1693, had opened its doors in 1698. It was to become a primary influence on the intellectual life of Colonial Virginia.

For four years, while the capitol building was under construction, the House of Burgesses met in the college building, "to the great disturbance of the college business," complained the president of the school.

Williamsburg became a lively, important city. Fairs were held often in Market Square, where farmers and craftsmen sold their wares. A broad main street extended between the capitol and the college. Bruton Parish Church stood near Market Square, and a wide green avenue led from the church to the Governor's Palace.

Taverns and boardinghouses soon sprang up in Williamsburg to take care of people who came there to study at the college, buy and sell merchandise, transact business at the courthouse, or take part in legislative sessions of the House of Burgesses.

THE COLONY GROWS AND PROSPERS

Virginia was the first colony established by the British, but it was not alone for long. By 1700, New Hampshire, Massachusetts, Connecticut, Rhode Island, New York, Pennsylvania, Maryland, and the Carolinas were all developing in their own directions.

Alexander Spotswood was governor of Virginia Colony from 1710 to 1722. He was a forward-looking and humane man who brought about some improvements in business and agriculture, encouraged settlement of western Virginia, and promoted fair treatment of blacks and Indians. For the next few decades, settlers poured into Virginia from other colonies as well as from abroad. By the end of the century, the population of Virginia had increased more than 1,000 percent, from about 70,000 in 1700 to more than 800,000 in 1800.

England was not the only European country interested in colonizing North America. Spain held some land in Florida. Dutch and Swedish settlers had come to New York and Delaware, but they had given up their claims early. France had a colony in Quebec and had established a number of fur-trading posts in the vicinity of the Great Lakes and the Mississippi River.

Colonel George Washington and his men raised the British flag after defeating the French at Fort Duquesne in 1758, during the French and Indian War.

France and England were in a race for control of the Ohio Valley, and their disputes led to the French and Indian War of 1754-63. It was in this war that a twenty-one-year-old Virginian, George Washington, began to take his place in the history of his state and his nation.

The French began to build a chain of forts between Lake Erie and the Ohio River. George Washington knew the territory; he had been a surveyor in the region. Governor Dinwiddie of Virginia sent the young man off to try to persuade the French to stop construction of the forts. When persuasion didn't work, Colonel Washington led a troop of 150 men in an attack on Fort Duquesne.

These were the opening shots of the French and Indian War. Washington won the first small skirmish, but was later defeated at Fort Necessity. However, with the help of the colonists, the British eventually won the war and ended all French claims in North America.

Chapter 5
THE REVOLUTIONARIES

THE REVOLUTIONARIES

Virginia came to play an enormously important role in the development of the nation. It was home to the visionaries who urged the colonists toward independence, successfully fought the Revolutionary War, and wrote the Constitution and the Bill of Rights.

Three of those visionaries, as different from one another as three men could possibly be, brought about some of the greatest accomplishments in world history.

PATRICK HENRY

Patrick Henry's leadership qualities were not readily apparent. Henry lived in a small community north of Richmond, in the Piedmont region of the state. He had failed at both farming and storekeeping. He preferred to go camping and hunting, or sit and chat with his backwoods friends, rather than apply himself to a money-making business. By the time he was twenty-four, he was married, the father of three children, and deeply in debt. He decided it was time to change his life, and chose law as his new career.

Patrick Henry studied law for a short time, and soon passed the bar examination given in Williamsburg. Within three years, he had made a name for himself as a passionate speaker in the courtroom.

Virginians—and citizens of other colonies as well—were beginning to chafe more and more under the restrictions imposed by the English government. The English kings and parliament looked on the colonies as sources of money and wealth for the English crown. They saw little advantage in giving rights to people an ocean away.

The colonists, on the other hand, considered themselves English citizens—who happened to live away from England. They felt entitled to the same rights as those granted to people living in England.

One issue, in particular, brought the difference in opinion into sharp focus—taxes. Colonists were not represented in Parliament, yet Parliament passed laws that allowed England to extract high taxes from the colonies. Lawyer Henry spoke eloquently in defense of the taxpayers of Virginia. In return, in 1765, he was elected to the House of Burgesses. He was twenty-nine years old.

GEORGE WASHINGTON

When George Washington came back from fighting in the French and Indian War in 1758, his fellow Virginians elected him to the House of Burgesses. He was twenty-six, and he served there for the next fifteen years.

Washington allowed other, more talkative, members to make the speeches and initiate the bills. He preferred to listen and watch attentively, absorbing an understanding of the legislative process.

Before his days as a soldier, Washington had been a farmer. But unlike Patrick Henry, Washington was a country gentleman from the Tidewater. He had inherited Mount Vernon, a good-sized estate. His wife also had large landholdings. Through his own efforts and business talent, Washington increased the value of his

George Washington's home, the beautiful estate called Mount Vernon, is located on the Potomac River near Alexandria.

assets considerably. He enjoyed entertaining his friends in traditional English style with events such as fox hunts.

Washington offered a stark contrast to Patrick Henry. Henry's style was that of a radical—impulsive and perhaps brash. Washington was deliberate and thoughtful—temperate in his judgments.

THOMAS JEFFERSON

Also in the House of Burgesses in Williamsburg during these crucial times was Thomas Jefferson. He had grown up in Shadwell, in Albemarle County, part of the rolling countryside of the western Piedmont near the Blue Ridge Mountains. His father, Peter Jefferson, had been a member of the House of Burgesses and a prominent and well-to-do farmer. His mother came from one of Virginia's oldest families, the Randolphs.

When Jefferson was fourteen, his father died, leaving him heir to a large farm and thirty slaves. Two years later, in 1759, Thomas Jefferson set off for Williamsburg to enter the College of William and Mary.

Jefferson thrived in the stimulating atmosphere. He graduated from college at nineteen and then studied law. After being admitted to the bar in 1767, Jefferson divided his time between Williamsburg and his home in Shadwell. He designed and supervised the construction of his own home, Monticello.

Thomas Jefferson was elected to the House of Burgesses in 1769. He was twenty-six years old. His talent with the written word soon became evident. Other burgesses asked for his help in writing laws and resolutions.

Jefferson had many prominent and aristocratic relatives and friends in the Tidewater. But he was also a son of the frontier. His ideas had been influenced by his boyhood neighbors, immigrant farmers who had worked hard to hack a living out of the wilderness. His political sympathies were more Piedmont than Tidewater. While still a law student, he had listened to Patrick Henry's fiery speech in protest of Britain's treatment of the colonists, and he was thrilled by it. Williamsburg was preparing a third revolutionary.

A CALL TO ACTION

Virginians were not the only colonists who felt a strong resentment against the numerous taxes. In December 1773, a group of Bostonians disguised as Indians met at the waterfront, seized 342 chests of English tea, and threw them into the bay—as a protest against a tax on tea. The Bostonians repeated their protest in March 1774.

In August 1774, the Virginia burgesses met at the Raleigh Tavern (left) to elect delegates to the First Continental Congress.

In an attempt to crush the Boston rebellion, the British closed the Port of Boston. The Virginia burgesses reacted to this news by deciding to set aside June 1 as a day to demonstrate their unity with the Bostonians. It was to be a day of fasting and prayer. The intention of the resolution was that the observation of those activities would "give us one heart and one mind firmly to oppose . . . every injury to American rights."

In an effort to stop the uprising's spread, Virginia's royal governor, Lord Dunmore, dissolved the House of Burgesses. The ploy did not work. The members of the assembly left the official meeting place and reconvened at the Raleigh Tavern. There the Virginians voted to send out a call for representatives from all the colonies to meet at a general congress.

Two months later, on August 1, the Virginia burgesses met once more at the Raleigh Tavern. At this meeting, called the First Virginia Convention, they elected seven delegates to what would be the First Continental Congress.

Chapter 6
FROM COLONY TO STATE

FROM COLONY TO STATE

On September 5, 1774, the First Continental Congress met in Philadelphia. Peyton Randolph of Virginia was chosen president of this convention of delegates from twelve colonies. Other Virginia delegates were George Washington, Patrick Henry, and Richard Henry Lee.

There was little talk of independence during this first session. The members hoped to persuade Parliament to change the tax and trade laws then in effect and to treat colonists as equals. If the colonists could not actually be represented in Parliament, they felt they should at least have the right to make their own laws.

England did not respond to the colonists' demands, and plans were made to hold a Second Continental Congress in May. In March, the Virginians held a Second Virginia Convention to elect delegates to the May meeting. This time the Virginians met in Richmond. There, in St. John's Episcopal Church, Patrick Henry made the best-remembered oration of his life. His words were an inspiration to everyone who heard or read them. He said, in part, " . . . there is no peace. The war is actually begun. . . . I know not what course others may take, but, as for me, give me liberty or give me death!"

It seemed that an open break with England was inevitable, and actual fighting began in Massachusetts in April of 1775. The Second Continental Congress, recognizing that a war had actually started (as Patrick Henry had declared a year earlier), organized

At the Second Virginia Convention, in May 1775, Patrick Henry made his famous "Give Me Liberty or Give Me Death!" speech.

an army and appointed George Washington its commander-in-chief. The Congress directed the separate colonies to act as independent states. They were held together only by their common cause, not by any kind of legal documents or agreements.

REVOLUTIONARY DOCUMENTS

While war was taking shape in the colonies, the Virginians had written a constitution. Virginia became an independent commonwealth on June 29, 1776, when its first constitution was adopted.

The Virginia constitution established two legislative houses and a weak executive branch. The governor was to be elected annually by the two houses of the legislature, and he could serve no more than three consecutive years. However, the most important part of

When Thomas Jefferson (right) drafted the Declaration of Independence, he used many of the ideas George Mason (above) had included in the Virginia constitution.

the new constitution of Virginia was its Bill of Rights, setting forth certain limits on a government's power to control private citizens.

Among other things, this document declared that "all men are by nature free and independent, and have certain inherent natural rights. . . ." and " . . . all power was originally lodged in and consequently is derived from the people." These ideas were penned by George Mason, who shunned public office, preferring to work behind the scenes. Mason's ideas found their way into the Declaration of Independence and the Bill of Rights in the United States Constitution as well as the Virginia constitution.

The American colonies, already fighting for their independence for more than a year, decided it was time to make a formal declaration, a legal separation from England. Virginia's Richard Henry Lee moved for a resolution of independence, and the Second Continental Congress appointed a committee to do the writing. Thomas Jefferson wrote most of the draft.

On July 4, 1776, John Hancock of Massachusetts, president of the Congress, signed the completed Declaration of Independence, and fifty-five members added their signatures later. Signers from Virginia were Francis Lightfoot Lee, Benjamin Harrison, Thomas Jefferson, Carter Braxton, and Thomas Nelson.

After the defeat of British troops at Yorktown in 1781, the captured flag was laid at the foot of Congress.

THE REVOLUTIONARY WAR IN VIRGINIA

During the Revolutionary War, battles were fought as far north as Canada and as far south as Georgia. Ironically, and in spite of the part Virginians had played before the fighting started, no battle occurred on Virginia soil until toward the end of the Revolution. British Major General Charles Cornwallis led his 9,750 soldiers into Virginia in late April 1781 and established a base at Yorktown, a short distance from Jamestown and Williamsburg. The French, meanwhile, had allied themselves with the Americans and had sent troops and ships to help the cause. In September, General Washington and an army of nearly 20,000 French and American troops arrived in Virginia and surrounded Yorktown. A fleet of French ships blockaded Chesapeake Bay to prevent Cornwallis from retreating. The defeat of the British troops at Yorktown climaxed a series of other victories by the American forces under Washington, and it proved to be the crucial one. When Britain's prime minister, Lord North, heard of the surrender by Cornwallis, he said, "Oh, God! It is all over."

Nearly two years later, a final peace treaty was signed. Britain gave up her claims to all the land from the Atlantic coast to the Mississippi River, and from what is now the United States-Canada border south to the lands still claimed by Spain.

CREATING A NEW GOVERNMENT

While the war was going on, the Continental Congress had appointed a committee to draft a set of Articles of Confederation and Perpetual Union. This was formally adopted by Congress, and ratified by the former colonies.

Each of the historical documents required negotiation and compromises. For example, in order to persuade Maryland to ratify the Articles of Confederation, Virginia agreed to give up its claims to the Northwest Territory. (Until this time, Virginia had claimed all the land included in the Virginia Company's charter.)

A few leaders, George Washington among them, began to see that this loose federation of states would not work well. Washington, along with his fellow Virginian James Madison and New Yorker Alexander Hamilton, were leaders of the Federalist cause. They wanted Congress to call a constitutional convention to establish the framework for a federal government.

Most of the former colonists still thought of themselves as Virginians or Pennsylvanians or New Yorkers, not as Americans. Their experiences with British kings and Parliament had made them suspicious of strong central governments.

The Continental Congress finally agreed to call a convention "for the sole and express purpose of revising the Articles of Confederation."

On September 17, 1787, delegates to the Constitutional Convention
gathered to sign the final draft of the United States Constitution.

After weeks of proposals and counterproposals, the delegates
decided to adopt a compromise plan. The plan called for two
houses of Congress, with equal representation of all states in one
and representation in proportion to population in the other. It
was agreed that the Constitution would take effect when nine
states had ratified it. Delaware was the first, and New Hampshire
was the ninth, on June 21, 1788.

VIRGINIA JOINS THE UNION

Virginia was not one of the first nine states. The Tidewater and
western regions of the state agreed with the new constitution. The
Piedmont section of the state favored a less-centralized form of
national government. Eventually, the Piedmont representative

On April 30, 1789, George Washington took the oath of office as the first president of the United States.

accepted the document on the condition that a bill of rights, like that in the Virginia constitution, be added. The Federalists promised to help pass amendments to the Constitution. On the strength of those promises, Virginia became the tenth state to join the Union, ratifying the Constitution on June 25, 1788.

To no one's surprise, George Washington was elected the new nation's first president. He was inaugurated on the steps of Federal Hall, in New York City, on April 30, 1789.

"I walk on untrodden ground," said President Washington as he started his duties as the head of a new nation with a new, precedent-setting constitution.

VIRGINIA'S LEGACY

Virginia is often called the "Mother of Presidents." Four of the nation's first five presidents were born there. John Adams, of Massachusetts, was elected the second president; he was followed, in succession, by three Virginians—Thomas Jefferson, James Madison, and James Monroe.

But Virginia provided more than presidents to the fledgling nation. John Marshall, a graduate of the College of William and Mary and veteran of the Virginia legislature, was nominated by President John Adams to serve as the third chief justice of the

Supreme Court. Marshall served on the court for more than thirty-four years. The court decisions made under his leadership made clear the structure of the federal government and the equality of its three branches. Many court decisions today are based on principles established by the Marshall Court.

During Jefferson's term of office, the territory of the young nation nearly doubled. The Louisiana Purchase pushed the country's borders westward from the Mississippi River to the Rocky Mountains. At the end of James Monroe's second term of office, in 1825, eleven new states had been admitted to the Union.

In 1841, Virginian William Henry Harrison was inaugurated president of the United States. He died after only a month in office, and was succeeded by Vice-President John Tyler, also from Virginia. Tyler's term, completed in 1845, marked the end of Virginia's preeminence in national politics.

Nevertheless, the list of Virginia's early governors who held office after the Revolutionary War reads like a Who's Who of the country's most famous patriots. Patrick Henry served from 1776 to 1779 and again from 1784 to 1786. Thomas Jefferson was the state's second chief executive. During the next few years, the office was occupied by Thomas Nelson, Jr., a signer of the Declaration of Independence; Benjamin Harrison, James Monroe, and John Tyler, Jr., all of whom later served as presidents of the United States; John Tyler, Sr., father of the future president; Edmund Randolph, member of the Continental Congress and of the Constitutional Convention; and Peyton Randolph, first president of the Continental Congress.

Many later Virginians achieved a respected place in history. However, Virginia's political contributions to the nation over a period of some eighty years stands without equal and is a great source of pride for Virginia's sons and daughters of today.

Chapter 7
CHANGE

CHANGE

While the momentous events leading to a new, independent nation were taking place in Virginia, changes in everyday life were occurring as well.

The state capital, moved from Jamestown to Williamsburg in 1698, was moved again in 1780. This time the capital was moved from the Tidewater city of Williamsburg to the Piedmont city of Richmond. In 1792, the state of Kentucky was formed from three of Virginia's western counties.

SCATTERED VIRGINIANS

In 1700, Virginia's population was about 70,000; by 1800, the population had swelled to 880,000. This population was scattered throughout the state rather than concentrated in cities or towns. In 1800, only 2.5 percent of the state's population lived in cities. This was due, in large part, to the plantation economy of the state. Plantations were relatively self-sufficient. They needed few goods or services from outside the plantation.

The self-sufficiency of the plantations had a significant effect on education in Virginia. Plantation owners could afford tutors for their children's education. They saw little reason to concern themselves with education for the poor.

About this time, the economics of Virginia began to change. The soils in the Tidewater and Piedmont had been exhausted from repeated plantings of tobacco. Cotton became the favored crop—a crop that brought in far less cash. In an effort to maintain or increase their wealth, some plantation owners turned to the slave trade as a source of income. Richmond, in the Piedmont, became the South's center of banking, flour milling, and manufacturing.

Meanwhile, the western regions of the state were developing. The land was unsuitable for tobacco or cotton, but its products of wheat, sheep, and iron had found ready markets. New immigrants and former indentured servants began settling in greater numbers in these western regions. Life there was not as grand as in the Tidewater, but there was a greater opportunity to start from nothing and succeed.

These ever-growing western counties agitated for greater representation in Virginia's government. In 1830 and 1851, the state adopted new constitutions, giving the west a greater voice in the general assembly. However, one of the westerners' main concerns—the cessation of slavery—went unaddressed.

FIRES OF REBELLION

Although Virginians had worked long and hard to establish "a more perfect union," they had failed to deal with the problem of gross inequality existing within the state. Washington, Jefferson, Madison, Mason, and Henry had all favored the emancipation of slaves. Yet the labor needs of the plantation, as well as the economics of slave trade, had forestalled any action toward freedom for slaves.

Occasionally, a slave rebelled against the cruel action of a ruthless master. Sometimes groups of slaves fought in anger to gain their freedom. In 1800, a Richmond slave named Gabriel planned to lead a thousand area slaves in an uprising. Though the

Nat Turner and his followers planning the 1831 revolt

action did not actually take place, Gabriel's Insurrection was a sign that slavery could not continue. In response to these revolts, whites increased the restrictions on slaves.

In 1831, Nat Turner led a particularly bloody revolt in Southside Virginia. Turner, a slave and a preacher, led several dozen slaves in a riot that resulted in the deaths of about sixty white people. Turner was captured and executed, and many other slaves were also killed in retaliation. Whites in the area reacted with fear and anger. It was no longer a way of life that was at stake. Turner's rebellion had taken white lives.

Individual slaveholders severely punished any slave who chanced to rebel. For its part, the state moved against abolitionists (those who wanted to abolish, or end, slavery). Members of the Abolitionist Society were forbidden to enter the state.

Two days after seizing a federal arsenal at Harpers Ferry in 1859, abolitionist John Brown was captured.

In 1859, John Brown, a rabid abolitionist, led a raid on the town of Harpers Ferry (in present-day West Virginia). He and a small group of men seized a federal arsenal and held several people hostage. In the process of seizing the arsenal, the group killed a freed black man. Some of Brown's followers tried to round up large numbers of slaves in the area in hope that they would start an insurrection. Shooting went on for two days. Brown was captured, and one of his sons was killed.

John Brown was tried, convicted, and executed for his crimes, and emotions on both sides of the slavery issue grew even more intense.

DIFFICULT CHOICES

The election of Abraham Lincoln to the presidency in 1860 was a signal to the South. Lincoln had already gone on record as being against slavery. If the southern states wished to continue their way of life, they would have to take some drastic steps. Slavery was not the only issue. Many southerners believed that they must take a stand for the right of states to make their own laws without interference from the federal government.

Even before Lincoln took office, seven southern states voted to secede from the Union. They formed their own separate government, the Confederate States of America. As Lincoln started his presidency, he stated that secession was illegal and that he would take steps to hold onto federal possessions in the South. One of these possessions was Fort Sumter, a military post in the harbor of Charleston, South Carolina.

On April 12, 1861, Confederate soldiers moved to seize the fort. Virginian Edmund Ruffin fired the first shell. Lincoln asked several states, Virginia among them, to provide forces to retaliate against the attack on the fort. Virginia refused to send its quota, and on April 14, Fort Sumter was forced to surrender. Virginia seceded from the Union on April 17, and on April 25 joined the Confederacy.

Many Virginians found their loyalties severely strained at this point. One, in particular, was Robert E. Lee. Lee was a graduate and former superintendent of West Point Academy, a member of one of Virginia's oldest families, and a colonel in the United States Army. He was not in favor of secession nor did he favor slavery. He had freed his own slaves years before. President Lincoln, knowing what Colonel Lee's beliefs were, asked him to take command of the Union army. But Lee was a Virginian, with strong roots and ties to his state. He resigned his commission and joined the Confederate army.

Many southerners were forced by circumstances to make the choice between their country and their state. Those who opted for the Confederacy felt they were fighting for the same liberties and legal principles for which their ancestors had fought during the American Revolution.

WEST VIRGINIA

Many of the people living in the mountains of Virginia, North Carolina, Kentucky, and Tennessee were opposed to the Confederate cause. They did not support slavery—they were too poor to own slaves. Many resented the wealthier landowners who lived down in the valleys and on the plateaus. The mountain people were a minority of the population, and they were so isolated that their influence in the distant state capital was weak. The Confederate cause widened the rift between Virginia's western counties and the Tidewater and Piedmont regions.

The fifty counties in Virginia's mountainous northwest region declared their independence from Virginia. At first, they called their state Kanawha, but soon changed it to West Virginia. West Virginia became the nation's thirty-fifth state on June 20, 1863.

THE CIVIL WAR IN VIRGINIA

The Revolutionary War had been fought mostly outside the borders of Virginia. The state was not as fortunate this time. From the beginning of the Civil War, Virginia was at the center of everything. Richmond had been named the capital of the Confederate States of America on May 21, 1861. Robert E. Lee took a major part in planning military strategy, and soon was made commander of the Army of Northern Virginia. The Civil War's first great battle, the First Battle of Manassas (called by northern forces the First Battle of Bull Run), was fought near Bull Run Creek. The South won its greatest victories on Virginia soil—Jackson's Valley Campaign, and the battles of Fredericksburg and Chancellorsville.

Other major battles fought in Virginia included Winchester,

The first great battle of the Civil War, called by southern forces the First Battle of Manassas and by northern forces the First Battle of Bull Run, was won by the South (above).

Richmond (shown at right as it looked in 1850) was the target of many Union attacks. Finally, in April 1865, when the capital of the Confederacy was moved, Richmond residents burned part of the city (below) so that it would be of little use to the Union. Mourning women (below right) later walked through the ruins of their city.

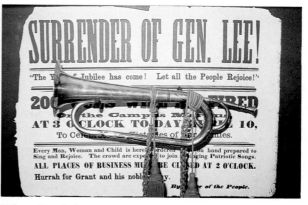

When Confederate General Robert E. Lee (left) surrendered to Union General Ulysses S. Grant, General George Custer's bugle (above) was sounded to mark the end of the Civil War.

Seven Pines (Fair Oaks), The Wilderness, New Market, Cold Harbor, Petersburg, and Lynchburg. The Shenandoah Valley, considered the "Granary of the Confederacy," was the site of fierce campaigns as the Union sought to undermine the Confederates' food supply. Richmond, the capital of the Confederacy, was another target of the Union forces, and great battles were waged there.

For four years the war raged on Virginia land, in and around Virginia farms and homes, fought by Virginia's Confederate sons. More battles were fought on Virginia soil than anywhere else. Of the war's approximately 4,000 battles, about 2,200 were fought in Virginia. Even the state's waters were not spared. The battle between the *Monitor* and the *Merrimac*, the first battle between two ironclad ships, was fought in Hampton Roads in 1862.

On April 25, 1865, General Robert E. Lee surrendered to General Ulysses S. Grant at Appomattox Court House. When General Lee returned to his troops to give them the sad news that the Confederacy had surrendered, he told them they had all done their best, but now it was time to go home, plant the crops, and obey the law. "If you make as good citizens as you have soldiers, you will do well, and I shall always be proud of you."

Chapter 8
INTO THE
TWENTIETH CENTURY

INTO THE TWENTIETH CENTURY

Recovery from the devastation of the Civil War was slow and difficult. Hundreds of thousands of southerners had died in battle or from disease. Businesses were bankrupt; the transportation system was in total collapse; and the state was staggering under a multimillion-dollar debt.

The emancipation of the slaves destroyed the old plantation system, a cornerstone of Virginia's economy. Slaves were now free, but almost all of them were homeless and jobless.

RECONSTRUCTION

After the war, the federal government passed the Reconstruction Act of 1867. The act provided military rule for the former state. It also called for a state constitutional convention to draw up a new constitution for Virginia. Nearly one-third of the convention delegates were black; the convention was controlled by Radical Republicans. The constitution, adopted in 1869, extended the right to vote to black males and provided for a statewide school system. Virginia was readmitted to the Union on January 26, 1870.

An overwhelming problem facing postwar Virginia was the state's tremendous debt. In prewar years, Virginia had borrowed money to finance canals, railroads, and turnpikes. With her

After the passage of the Reconstruction Act, black males were permitted to vote.

economy in shambles, Virginia was clearly unable to repay the
$47 million. The interest alone, nearly $3 million, was more than
the state's entire budget had been in many prewar years.

Many felt that to refinance the state debt was to lessen
Virginia's pride. Others felt that without a readjustment in the
debt, Virginia would never be able to rebuild the railroads, farms,
ports, and cities that had been destroyed during the war. The
legislature worked with the state's creditors to have the debt
reduced to $27 million, a figure more in keeping with the state's
ability to pay.

The work of black legislators resulted in the repeal of the poll
tax in the early 1880s. A poll tax was an amount of money each
taxpayer was required to pay in order to register to vote. It was
used in many cases as a way of preventing poor people—and in
the postwar South, that included most blacks—from voting.

Among the educational institutions for blacks that were founded by the Freedmen's Bureau were the Misses Cooke's School in Richmond (left) and the Hampton Normal and Industrial Institute (right).

BLACKS IN POSTWAR VIRGINIA

At the close of the war, Congress set up the Freedmen's Bureau, an agency to help freed slaves with relief supplies and other assistance. The agency existed for only seven years, but it was successful in helping to start several educational institutions for blacks.

Education became a priority. In Hampton, Virginia, lessons in basic reading and writing were held under a tree known as the Emancipation Oak. Men, women, and children attended. General Samuel Chapman Armstrong, an agent of the Freedmen's Bureau, decided that Hampton would be a "strategic spot for a permanent and great educational work." He persuaded the American Missionary Association to start a more formal school. Land was purchased and classes began in 1868. Armstrong was named the first principal of the Hampton Normal and Industrial Institute, now called Hampton University.

Hampton University (above) and St. Paul's College (right), are among the post-Civil War schools for blacks that grew into full-fledged colleges and universities.

Hampton's most famous student was Booker T. Washington, a former slave whose influence on the education of blacks was enormous. He organized the Tuskegee Institute in Alabama in 1881 and served as its president until 1915.

Several other schools for blacks, started in the postwar years, grew into full-fledged colleges and universities that still exist today. Virginia Union University, in Richmond, which grew from a school first established by Northern Baptists in 1865, held its first classes in a building formerly used to jail rebellious slaves. The cells were used as classrooms, and the whipping post was made into a lectern (a reading desk). A state-supported school— Virginia Normal and Collegiate Institute—was founded in 1882 in Petersburg. Today it is called Virginia State College. St. Paul's College in Lawrenceville was founded by the Episcopal Church in 1882.

At the turn of the century, gains made by blacks began to slip away. Legal segregation in public places, unknown in Virginia until about 1900, began when the state legislature passed a law requiring blacks and whites to sit in separate railroad cars.

Discrimination in other public services soon followed. Separate schools for blacks and whites were established.

In 1902, a new state constitution was adopted, one that included new requirements for voting. The poll tax was reestablished, and people registering to vote had to pass a test on the constitution. Local election boards were able to set up tests in any way they chose and ask any questions they wished. These measures were a means of eliminating the political power of blacks. They severely reduced the number of blacks who were able to vote and nearly ended black participation in Virginia politics.

Not until the Civil Rights Movement of the 1960s did these unjust conditions change.

VIRGINIA'S INDUSTRIAL REVOLUTION

Virginia had been prosperous in pre-Civil War days. One of the major factors in its prosperity was the excellent railroad system. Railroads had first come into Virginia in the 1830s, and at the beginning of the war, one-sixth of the nation's total track was in that state.

The war left the transportation system in terrible condition, but by the 1880s, the railroads once again were helping the state to recover. Roanoke, in western Virginia, grew from a settlement of seven hundred people to a city of five thousand in two years when two important railroads established a junction there.

It was also in the 1880s that rich deposits of coal were discovered in southwestern Virginia. The Norfolk and Western Railway was ideally situated to haul the product across the state for shipment. The first carload was taken to Norfolk in 1883. Today, the port of Norfolk has the largest coal-loading piers in the world.

Newport News became a port city terminus for handling coal from West Virginia. Soon Virginia's shipbuilding industry blossomed, also centered in Newport News.

New manufacturing in this period included cotton textiles and furniture. A new variety of bright-leaf tobacco was developed, and the tobacco-processing and cigarette-manufacturing plants near Richmond expanded. The use of chemical fertilizers made it possible for farmers to grow other crops on land that had been considered worthless for anything except tobacco.

Though Virginia achieved nearly complete economic recovery by the end of the nineteenth century, it continued to be a comparatively poor state until the first World War.

HARRY FLOOD BYRD

World War I brought a new prosperity to Virginia. New factories, munitions plants, and military training centers sprang up in the state in response to the national needs.

At the close of the war, a young state senator named Harry Flood Byrd was coming into prominence in Virginia. He was destined to be the most important political figure in the state for the next forty-five years. He was elected governor of Virginia in 1926 and served until 1930.

Governor Byrd's administration was one of reform. Under his leadership, the state bureaucracy was streamlined, the tax structure was revised, and mental hospitals, roads, and schools were improved. He worked hard to establish Shenandoah National Park. New businesses were attracted to Virginia as a result of tax reforms. The state treasury had a deficit when Byrd took office, and even though taxes were reduced during his administration, there was a surplus when he left office.

These soldiers at Camp Belvoir used dummy guns to train for service in World War I.

Lynchings, all too common at the time, were the South's biggest disgrace. White mobs would go on a rampage with little or no excuse, find and seize a black victim, and hang him from the branch of a tree until he was dead. Governor Byrd, determined to end this terror in Virginia, led passage of a strong antilynching bill in 1928. There have been no lynchings in Virginia since then.

THE 1930s

In 1929, when the Great Depression started, Virginia was more prosperous than any of the other former Confederate states. The economy was relatively well balanced, depending on a mix of agriculture, manufacturing, and commerce. Farming had become more diversified than in many other states. The percentage of the state's residents who owned their own homes was higher than the national average.

People in Richmond and Norfolk were better off than in the rest of the state. Richmond's economy was well balanced, and Norfolk's was greatly helped by the large navy base.

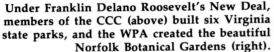
Under Franklin Delano Roosevelt's New Deal, members of the CCC (above) built six Virginia state parks, and the WPA created the beautiful Norfolk Botanical Gardens (right).

Nevertheless, the state suffered greatly, along with the rest of the country. A catastrophic drought in the summer of 1930 destroyed many crops. A strike in a textile mill in Danville ended in a defeat for the workers; many of them lost their jobs permanently. Thousands of children could not go to school because their parents could not afford to buy them shoes and clothing.

Under President Franklin Delano Roosevelt's leadership, Congress initiated several emergency measures in an attempt to cope with the nation's economic crisis. His program was known as the New Deal.

Several New Deal projects resulted in lasting benefit to Virginia. The Works Project Administration (WPA) sponsored the creation of beautiful azalea gardens in Norfolk that still delight visitors. The Public Works Administration (PWA) built the Virginia State Library, a library at the University of Virginia, a hospital at the Medical College of Virginia, and many other public buildings. The Rural Electrification Administration (REA) brought electricity to thousands of Virginia farms. In 1934, less than 8 percent of the state's farmers had electricity; within the next fourteen years, nearly all farms were electrified.

The Civilian Conservation Corps (CCC) put thousands of young unemployed men—both white and black—to work building bridges and doing conservation work. Six of Virginia's state parks were built by the CCC..

INDUSTRIAL EXPANSION

Virginia was the nation's most important arsenal during World War II, which lasted from 1941 to 1945. About fifty armed-service installations were located within the state.

The population of Norfolk doubled almost overnight as the navy built up its strength. The nearby cities of Portsmouth and Newport News also boomed. Army camps and marine bases expanded almost as rapidly. Radford, in the mountains of western Virginia, brought in some twenty thousand new employees to work in a huge munitions plant.

Many people stationed in Virginia during the war made their permanent homes in the state after the war. Industry, particularly the manufacture of chemicals, clothing, electrical equipment, and transportation equipment, continued to expand. The state legislature adopted an aggressive plan to recruit new industry, and in 1964 passed a variety of tax incentives for that purpose. Also in 1964, the $200 million Chesapeake Bay Bridge-Tunnel, linking the Virginia mainland with the Eastern Shore, was completed.

THE CIVIL RIGHTS MOVEMENT

Slavery in Virginia has always been a source of controversy. Even in 1619, there were people who believed that slavery and racism were morally wrong and that all races were entitled to equal treatment. Others sincerely believed in white supremacy. The Civil War did not lessen these differences. During Reconstruction, blacks achieved some political power in the South, but by the end of the nineteenth century, that power had been eliminated. Until World War II, the inferior position of blacks in southern society was not challenged in any effective way.

After World War II, black soldiers returning to civilian life in the South were anxious to achieve full equality. They had risked their lives along with white servicemen to preserve the American way of life, and they wanted to share in that way of life.

A milestone in the struggle for civil rights occurred in 1954, when the United States Supreme Court's decision in the *Brown v. Board of Education of Topeka* case pointed the way to ending racial segregation in public schools. Virginia's politicians, including Senator Byrd and Governor Thomas V. Stanley, were determined to continue the segregation system.

For the next ten years, Virginia's political leaders tried by various means to avoid integrating the public schools. New private schools were organized in some localities, and many white students left the public school system entirely. Some schools were closed; those in Prince Edward County were closed from 1958 to 1964. The first public schools in Virginia to be integrated were in Norfolk and Arlington, in 1959.

In spite of many legal maneuvers and widespread resistance to integration, Virginia, unlike many other states, eventually achieved a transition without violence.

The political climate changed gradually. In 1964, the state poll tax was eliminated and in 1977, Richmond elected its first black mayor. In 1985, L. Douglas Wilder was elected lieutenant governor, the first black to be elected to a major state office since Reconstruction.

Chapter 9

GOVERNMENT
AND THE ECONOMY

GOVERNMENT AND THE ECONOMY

Virginia has prospered in recent years. Its economy is diversified, with strong elements of government employment, manufacturing, commerce, mining, tourism, agriculture, and fishing.

The twentieth century has seen a great shift in the ways that most Virginians make a living. More than half the residents of the state were engaged in agriculture in 1900. By 1970, fewer than 3 percent were still on the farms.

GOVERNMENT

Virginia is officially called a commonwealth, a term referring to a nation or state governed by the people. Virginia's first state constitution was adopted in 1776. It set an example for many other states and established several important principles, especially those expressed in the Bill of Rights.

Revised constitutions were adopted in 1830, 1851, 1869, 1902, and 1971. Even though there have been several revisions to the state's constitution, some of the wording is as it was in 1776, indicating that Virginia's early leaders had developed a truly timeless document. Over the years, voting privileges have been extended to more and more people, and the authority invested in state government has increased while the authority of the counties has decreased. The power of the executive branch (the office of the governor) has been strengthened considerably.

The governor is responsible for enforcing, or carrying out, the laws. In Virginia, the governor has more power than in many other states. He appoints most state officials. He has veto power over bills passed by the legislative branch (the General Assembly), and can veto individual items in money bills.

The legislative branch is responsible for making and repealing laws. Virginia's General Assembly consists of two legislative houses, the senate and the house of delegates. Members are elected in odd-numbered years and meet each January. Sessions are scheduled for sixty days in even-numbered years and for thirty days in odd-numbered years, but can be extended for up to thirty days. Also, the governor can call special sessions.

The judicial branch (the court system) interprets the laws. Justices of the state supreme court and judges of circuit courts are selected by the General Assembly. Justices serve twelve-year terms; judges are elected for eight years and may be reappointed by the General Assembly. Virginia also has an appeals court that handles appeals from the lower courts.

There are 95 counties, 41 independent cities, and 189 incorporated towns in Virginia. When an area is incorporated as a city, it is no longer considered to be part of the county. This can get somewhat confusing. For example, there is a Roanoke city and a Roanoke county, and the city is independent of the county. Also, Charles City is a county name; there is no city with that name.

EDUCATION

Because Jamestown was the first permanent white settlement in the nation, Virginia is the site of some of the nation's first schools. The Syms Free School in Hampton was established in 1634; the Eaton Free School began about 1640. The College of William and

Above: The Lee-Jackson House on the Washington and Lee University campus in Lexington
Right: The Wren Building at the College of William and Mary in Williamsburg

Mary, founded in 1693, is the nation's second-oldest institution of higher learning; only Harvard was started earlier. Other long-standing Virginia schools include Washington and Lee University, founded in 1749; Hampden-Sydney College, founded in 1776; and the University of Virginia in Charlottesville, founded by Thomas Jefferson in 1819.

The scattered population patterns as well as the plantation way of life frustrated the establishment of a statewide public school system. It was not until 1870 that such a system was established, offering education on an equal basis to both white and black students. Although the system was established during Reconstruction, it was 1902 before the state constitution provided for funding. By that time, Virginia's extensive Civil War debts and segregationist practices kept the state's dollar contribution to the schools below average, and it remained so until the 1960s.

In the 1970s, the state board of education took active measures to improve the education of Virginia's school-age children. In the late 1980s, the average score of Virginia students on national tests exceeded the national average. More than two-thirds of the state's graduates go on to higher education. A decade earlier, only half the students pursued higher education.

Millions of tons of cargo are moved through Virginia's port areas of Newport News, Norfolk, Portsmouth, and Chesapeake. Shipbuilding and ship-repairing yards such as this one in the Norfolk-Portsmouth area are major Virginia employers.

Twenty-three community colleges in Virginia, located on thirty-three campuses, provide job training, retraining, and courses that are transferable to four-year colleges. Four-year programs are offered at twelve state-supported and twenty-seven privately supported colleges and universities.

TRANSPORTATION

Virginia's location makes it an ideal transportation center, since about half of all the people in the United States live within a 500-mile (805-kilometer) radius of Richmond. The state's transportation network is excellent. There are about 55,000 miles (88,512 kilometers) of surfaced roads and highways. Four interstate routes cross the state from north to south, and two cross the state from east to west. The Chesapeake Bay Bridge-Tunnel connects the mainland with the Eastern Shore.

Thirteen railroads provide rail freight service, and Amtrak provides passenger rail service.

Millions of tons of cargo for foreign trade are moved through Virginia's port areas, including Norfolk, Newport News, Portsmouth, and Chesapeake.

Commercial fishing for oysters, crabs, scallops, and clams is an important industry in Virginia. Seafood lovers in the East and elsewhere are delighted when they find blue crabs (above) on a restaurant menu.

Virginia is served by twelve airports within the state, three in the Washington metropolitan area, one in West Virginia, and one in Tennessee.

COMMUNICATION

Of the nearly 140 newspapers that are published in Virginia, 36 are dailies. Those with the largest circulation are the Norfolk *Virginia Pilot,* the *Richmond News Leader,* the Roanoke *Times & World News,* and the *Richmond Times-Dispatch.* There are 251 radio stations and 48 television stations in the state.

AGRICULTURE AND FISHING

Improved technology and the use of machinery have kept the value of agricultural products at a high level. In the 1980s, agriculture accounted for 1 percent of the state's gross product.

Tobacco provides more income for Virginia than any other crop. Shown here is a Wise County tobacco field being harvested.

Although tobacco is still an important crop in Virginia, providing more income than any other crop, the state is no longer dependent on a single crop.

Large quantities of vegetables and fruits are grown on the truck farms of the Eastern Shore. Peanuts, soybeans, and hogs are produced in the section immediately west of Norfolk; Smithfield hams, famous throughout the world, are a product of that area. Wheat, corn, and dairy products are important in northern Virginia.

The Shenandoah Valley is one of the most important regions in the country for growing apples. Poultry raising, particularly turkey farming, is an important industry there as well. Cattle are raised in several parts of central and western Virginia.

Chesapeake Bay is famous for its seafood, especially for its oysters and crabs. Commercial fishing for scallops and clams in the bay and the ocean is an important industry. Menhaden, an inedible fish, is processed for oil and fertilizer.

SERVICE AND MANUFACTURING

In Virginia, service industries—such as government, community and social services, and wholesale and retail trade—employ nearly 5 percent of the state's workers.

More people work for the government than for any other industry; in the 1980s, about 22 percent of Virginia's workers held jobs with the state or federal governments.

Manufacturing, construction, and mining provide 24 percent of the state's gross product. Tobacco products are among the state's most important products. Chemical products, including synthetic fibers such as nylon, and drug manufacture are major sources of income for the state.

The Newport News Shipbuilding and Dry Dock Company is the state's largest private employer and provides the nucleus for the world's largest shipbuilding and ship-repair yards.

NATURAL RESOURCES

An abundant water supply, a lack of serious air pollution problems, and a moderate climate are among the state's natural assets. About 60 percent of the land is forested, nearly all of it capable of producing commercial timber. About a thousand processing plants in the state handle forest products.

The coalfields of southwestern Virginia are still important to the state's economy. Production and prices fluctuate with world prices of oil, but in the late 1980s, Virginia was producing more than $1.5 billion worth of coal each year.

Granite, limestone, marble, and shale are quarried in the state. Other mineral resources include gypsum, kyanite, iron oxides, and zinc.

Virginia's excellent recreational facilities, as well as the numerous historical sites in the state, are major tourist attractions. Many tourists are especially interested in the reconstructed colonial capital of Williamsburg (left).

TOURISM

Tourism brings a great deal of income to Virginia each year. The state is within one day's drive of much of the population of the East Coast, with both mountains and seashore easily accessible. Recreational facilities include twenty-six state parks, as well as regional and national parks, nine major lakes, scenic parkways, a national seashore, and many wildlife refuges. The state's forests provide thousands of miles of hiking trails. More than 1,500 miles (2,414 kilometers) of shoreline give both residents and tourists unlimited access to saltwater sports.

Equally impressive is the number of historic sites. The homes of several presidents, more than a half-dozen historic battlefields, and the finest restoration area in the world—Colonial Williamsburg—are only part of the story. Markers along the highways and identifying plaques on historic buildings abound. One of the roadside markers is at Front Royal, honoring a man named William E. Carson. His chief claim to fame is that he started the practice of calling attention to Virginia's hundreds of historic sites—by installing roadside markers at appropriate spots!

Chapter 10
CULTURE AND RECREATION

CULTURE AND RECREATION

Virginia offers a wide range of cultural achievements and recreational activities that reach beyond history and politics.

LITERATURE

Virginia's best-known literary figure is Edgar Allan Poe—poet, critic, editor, and master of mysterious and eerie short stories. His first short stories were published in *The Southern Literary Messenger*, a Richmond literary magazine of which Poe later became editor. Among Poe's best-known works are his poems "The Raven," "Ulalume," and "Annabel Lee," and his short stories "The Gold Bug," "The Murders in the Rue Morgue," and "The Fall of the House of Usher." Though Poe was born in Boston, he spent much of his life in Richmond and always called himself a Virginian.

Several Virginia writers achieved success and fame in the 1930s. Three of them lived in Richmond—Ellen Glasgow, James Branch Cabell, and Douglas Southall Freeman. Glasgow had very little formal education, but she read widely. Her novels about upper-class society in Virginia were so true to life that critics have called them "social history." One of them, *In This Our Life*, won a Pulitzer Prize.

James Branch Cabell, a graduate of the College of William and Mary, was a friend and neighbor of Ellen Glasgow. He was a newspaperman before he started writing novels. Many of Cabell's novels were set in an imaginary medieval country.

Douglas Southall Freeman was editor of the *Richmond News Leader* for more than thirty years. Best remembered for his biographies, he was awarded Pulitzer Prizes for *R.E. Lee* (1935) and *George Washington* (volumes 1-6) (1958).

A more recent Virginia writer, Earl Hamner, created two enormously successful, long-running television series, "The Waltons" and "Falcon Crest." The Waltons are a fictionalized family closely based on Hamner's own; many of the plots grew out of his own experiences in Virginia as a child and young man. The stories center on the warmth and sharing of a struggling southern family.

PERFORMING ARTS

Deep in the mountains of southwestern Virginia, a town of about four thousand people is famous in the world of the theater.

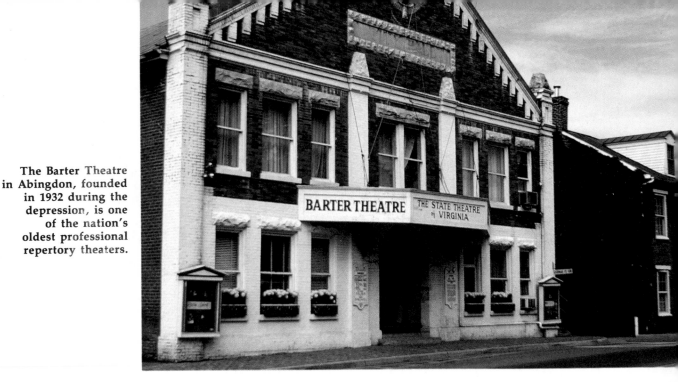

The Barter Theatre in Abingdon, founded in 1932 during the depression, is one of the nation's oldest professional repertory theaters.

In 1932, native Virginian Bob Porterfield brought a group of actors to Abingdon. The depression had dimmed many of the lights on Broadway and the two dozen men and women were desperately looking for a way to practice their craft. Porterfield had an idea. People in and around Abingdon had food, but no money, so at the Barter Theatre, a variety of items such as hams, vegetables, jellies, and apples could be exchanged for tickets. Nine out of ten tickets were swapped for food in those days. The theater managed to stay afloat for fourteen years, and the actors were able to eat. In 1946, Virginia's General Assembly voted a fund of $10,000 for the project, and the Barter Theatre became the first state-supported theater in the nation. Today, the theater's season runs from April to October. It is one of the nation's oldest professional repertory theaters.

Theatre Virginia is another professional repertory theater company; its home base is the Virginia Museum of Fine Arts in Richmond.

Performing-arts centers in Richmond, Norfolk, Portsmouth,

Virginia Beach, and Roanoke host various outstanding programs. The John F. Kennedy Center for the Performing Arts, just across the Potomac River in Washington, draws large numbers of people from Virginia.

Eight Virginia communities have symphony orchestras. Norfolk has an opera company, a stage company, and a philharmonic orchestra. Richmond's symphony orchestra presents pops, operatic, ballet, chamber, and choral music as well as symphonic programs. The Richmond Sinfonia performs throughout the state, and travels outside Virginia as well.

Wolf Trap Farm Park for the Performing Arts, in Vienna, near Washington, is a community of theaters offering opera, musical concerts, dance programs, and dramatic presentations in a spectacular setting. The park is owned and run by the National Park System and is the only one of its kind.

Music festivals are popular in the mountain towns. One of the best is the Old Fiddlers' Convention, held each August in Galax. The Blue Ridge Folklife Festival, held in Ferrum in October, features traditional gospel, blues, and string band music.

Hampton University has been famous for its choir for more than a century. In 1870, the group made a concert tour that raised enough money to build a college hall.

SPORTS AND RECREATION

The National Football League Washington Redskins team is headquartered in Loudoun County, Virginia. It is the only professional sports team in the state. Virginians also root for the American League Baltimore Orioles baseball team. But their most enthusiastic loyalties are for the state's various college and university football and basketball teams.

Horses play a large part in the lives of many Virginians. Fox hunts are held regularly (left), and the annual Chincoteague pony roundup and sale (above) draws tourists as well as buyers.

Sailing regattas and surfing competitions attract audiences to the coast. Thoroughbred horse shows are popular in parts of the state. Northern Virginia and parts of central Virginia are "horse country," and English-style fox hunts are held there regularly.

A most unusual sport takes place annually on the Eastern Shore. Chincoteague ponies run wild here, on Assateague Island National Seashore. During the last week in July, known as Pony Penning Week, a roundup is held and a certain number of the ponies are offered for sale.

More than 2 million acres (.8 million hectares) of public lands are available for recreation in the state of Virginia. Twenty-six state parks are scattered over the state, and more are being developed. Some are still rather rustic, but at least two-thirds of the parks have facilities such as campgrounds, cabins, hiking trails, boat launches, areas for swimming and fishing, concessions, and interpretive programs.

Midsummer raft races on the Rappahannock River attract fun-loving crowds.

Water sports are enjoyed on nine major lakes and dozens of smaller ones, as well as on rivers and streams. There are 450 public fishing streams. The shoreline of Virginia is about 1,500 miles (2,414 kilometers) long, with frontage on the Atlantic Ocean, Chesapeake Bay, and tidal estuaries. This makes it one of the best areas anywhere for saltwater sports.

The federal government manages Shenandoah National Park, Assateague National Seashore, Chincoteague National Wildlife Refuge, Mount Rogers National Recreational Area, and Prince William Forest Park, as well as nine historic sites. There are three national scenic parkways in the state in addition to the Skyline Drive, which is in Shenandoah National Park. They are the Blue Ridge Parkway, Colonial Parkway, and George Washington Memorial Parkway.

Serious hikers all know about the Appalachian National Scenic Trail, a mountain trail that runs from Maine to Georgia. It includes a long stretch across Virginia's mountains, entering the state east of Winchester and continuing to the North Carolina line near Mount Rogers.

Chapter 11
A GRAND TOUR OF VIRGINIA

A GRAND TOUR OF VIRGINIA

"I have been planning what I would show you: a flower here, a tree there; yonder a grove, near it a fountain; on this side a hill, on that a river. Indeed, madam, I know nothing so charming as our own country."

Thomas Jefferson wrote those words to a friend in London in 1788. There is much in Virginia he would not recognize today, but he would still find it charming. He would be pleased to find that his old haunts in Williamsburg, his beloved Monticello, and several landmarks at his University of Virginia have been lovingly preserved.

Few states offer such a wealth of delights to sightseers: historic and natural landmarks, recreational and educational facilities, and just beautiful places to visit.

NORTHERN VIRGINIA

After the Revolutionary War, the Continental Congress recognized they must find a permanent home for the federal government. After much negotiating, a compromise was reached. A ten-mile (sixteen-kilometer) square along the Potomac River, a little more than half of it to be donated by the state of Maryland and the rest by Virginia, would be a federal district, not a part of either state. George Washington selected the precise location.

A memorial ceremony at the Tomb of the Unknowns in Arlington National Cemetery

In 1846, the federal government decided it didn't need that much space, so Virginia's contribution, the section south of the river, was given back to the state.

Arlington County, which was within the original boundaries of the federal district, is twenty-five square miles (sixty-five square kilometers) packed with a collection of neighborhoods and housing developments. Thousands of government workers and people who do business with the government live here and in Alexandria, also once part of the district.

Arlington National Cemetery contains the graves of more than two hundred thousand men and women who have served the country in various ways. The cemetery is the final resting place of nearly twenty thousand soldiers of the Civil War. The Tomb of the Unknowns contains the remains of four unidentified American soldiers—one who was killed during World War I, one during

Old Prince Street, paved with cobblestones, is the oldest street in historic Alexandria.

World War II, one during the Korean War, and one during the Vietnam War.

President William Howard Taft's grave is here, as are those of President John F. Kennedy and his brother Robert.

Also within the cemetery is Arlington House, the home of Robert E. Lee for thirty years before the Civil War.

The Pentagon, the largest office building in the world, is in Arlington. Guided tours are available of this huge building, headquarters of the United States Department of Defense.

West of Arlington is Wolf Trap Farm Park, where wonderful concerts and dramatic programs are presented year-round. Nearby, on the Potomac River, is Great Falls Park, a large park with deep woods, a picturesque swamp, and roaring waterfalls.

Alexandria has cobblestone streets and many pre-Revolutionary townhouses. The lovely old buildings are used for homes, shops,

Reston, near Dulles
International Airport,
is a completely
planned city built
after World War II.

restaurants, and museums. There are several mansions and
plantation homes nearby. One of them—Gunston Hall—was the
home of George Mason.

Also near Alexandria is George Washington's Mount Vernon,
located on the banks of the Potomac River. Thousands of visitors
come here every year to walk through the house, outbuildings,
and gardens. Many original pieces of furniture and other
possessions of the first president are on display.

Reston is a completely planned city built after World War II. It
is close to Dulles International Airport, one of the world's busiest.
Northwest of here, along the Potomac River, the countryside
changes from suburban to rural, with gently rolling hills. White
fences mark farms where thoroughbred horses are raised.

Leesburg, founded in 1758, is the site of several colonial
restorations. At a mansion called Morven Park is a museum

Dulles International Airport

containing more than a hundred horse-drawn vehicles. Just west of town is the American Work Horse Museum, with thousands of objects related to horses and the work they have done.

South of Leesburg is Manassas National Battlefield Park, the site of two major Civil War battles. This is where General Thomas Jackson got his nickname, "Stonewall." The legend is that someone in the Confederate forces rallied the men behind him by crying, "Look! There stands Jackson like a stone wall. Rally behind the Virginians!" The South won battles at this site in 1861 and 1862. The exhibits and presentation at the visitor center tell the story of the battles.

Fredericksburg is a charming, historic city, about half-way between Washington and Richmond. Its landmarks reflect both the Revolutionary and Civil War periods. George Washington's mother and sister both lived here; their homes can be visited. James Monroe's law office, also located here, has been preserved. It is furnished with pieces he brought back from France in 1794.

The Fredericksburg and Spotsylvania National Military Park memorializes four major battles of the Civil War.

In 1619, Berkeley Plantation was the site of the first Thanksgiving in North America.

TIDEWATER

Petersburg is part of Tidewater Virginia. Like Fredericksburg, it is a storehouse of history from the colonial, revolutionary, and Civil War periods. It was occupied by British troops during the Revolutionary War and was the site of Lee's last stand before his surrender at Appomattox Court House.

Along the James River is a collection of plantations that have survived for more than 250 years. One of them, Shirley, counts nine generations of the Carter family as its owners. Robert E. Lee, a relative of the Carters, spent part of his boyhood here.

Berkeley Plantation was the home of Benjamin Harrison IV and his wife, Anne Carter. They were the grandparents of President William Henry Harrison, who was born at Berkeley, and great-great-grandparents of President Benjamin Harrison. The buildings and grounds have undergone extensive restoration. Berkeley was the site of the first Thanksgiving in North America, in the fall of 1619.

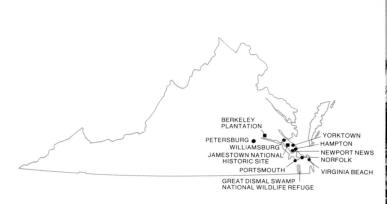

Costumed dancers at
Busch Gardens-The Old
Country, a family theme
park near Williamsburg

Sherwood Forest, the home of the tenth president, John Tyler, marks the beginning of the Virginia Peninsula, a strip of land between the James and York rivers. The historic area—including Williamsburg, Jamestown, and Yorktown—is often called the Colonial Triangle.

Williamsburg was the site of many historic events. The central part of the modern city of Williamsburg is still very much like it was in the 1700s. At the reconstructed colonial capital, artisans and innkeepers are costumed as eighteenth-century colonials, giving the area an aura of "living history." Visitors can watch artisans demonstrating such colonial crafts as silversmithing, weaving, making pottery, and shoeing horses. In the restored taverns they can eat the foods the colonists ate. They can smell the fragrances of the eighteenth-century herb and flower gardens, hear the sounds of old-fashioned instruments, and touch the walls of buildings that have stood since before the Revolution.

Busch Gardens-The Old Country, is nearby. This family theme park complements the colonial history of Williamsburg by giving visitors the flavor of some of the European countries from which many of the early settlers came.

The original settlement of Jamestown no longer exists as a town. Jamestown National Historic Site is in about the same natural state the first settlers found when they got off the boats. Interpretive programs at the visitors' center tell the story and describe the conditions the pioneers faced. Next to the national site is Jamestown Festival Park, with a re-creation of the original James Fort of 1607 and a Powhatan Indian village of the type the settlers might have seen. Three full-sized replicas of the original boats lie at anchor, *Susan Constant*, *Godspeed*, and *Discovery*.

Yorktown is the site of the final victory of the American Revolution. The story of the war and the last battle is told at the Yorktown Battlefield Visitor Center and the Yorktown Victory Center. Outside is a replica of a Revolutionary War encampment.

The cities of Hampton and Newport News are at the tip of the Virginia Peninsula. Across a deep-water harbor at the mouth of the James River, known as Hampton Roads, are Portsmouth and Norfolk.

Hampton is one of Virginia's earliest settlements. It saw a great deal of action during the Revolutionary War. Langley Air Force

Base, Fort Monroe, and the Langley Research Center for the National Aeronautics and Space Administration (NASA) are here. The NASA Visitor Center includes an excellent space museum.

Newport News, adjacent to Hampton, faces the James River. The Newport News Shipbuilding Company is the largest of its kind in the world. The War Memorial Museum of Virginia displays more than sixty thousand artifacts from all the military conflicts in American history. The Mariners Museum is one of the finest of its kind in the United States. Dedicated to maritime history, it has outstanding collections of ship models and miniatures, marine paintings, and marine decorative arts.

Norfolk is Virginia's largest city. The Norfolk Naval Base and the Atlantic headquarters of the North Atlantic Treaty Organization (NATO) make up the largest naval installation in the country. The Waterside Festival Marketplace is a complex of shops and restaurants on the Elizabeth River. Two of the city's most popular attractions are the International Azalea Festival, held each year in April, and Harborfest, held in June. Also worth seeing in Norfolk are the Botanical Gardens and the Chrysler Art Museum.

Portsmouth is home of the Portsmouth Naval Shipyard Museum, the Portsmouth Lightship Museum, and the U.S. Naval Hospital.

East of Norfolk, on the Atlantic Ocean, is Virginia Beach. This is a very different world from the busy ports nearby. Dedicated to summer recreation, there are dozens of beachfront hotels and motels, restaurants, a long public beach, a concrete boardwalk, and fine facilities for surfing, swimming, fishing, boating, waterskiing, biking, tennis, and golf.

Below the James River, away from the big cities, are the small hamlets, pine woods, and countryside of Southside Virginia. Near

The Chesapeake Bay Bridge-Tunnel as seen from Norfolk

the North Carolina border is the Great Dismal Swamp, a large refuge for birds and small animals.

EASTERN SHORE

The part of Virginia called the Eastern Shore, located on Delmarva Peninsula, is completely separated by water from the rest of the state. The Chesapeake Bay Bridge-Tunnel makes it possible to drive from the vicinity of Norfolk and Virginia Beach, on the mainland, across to the peninsula. This impressive transportation link is the world's longest bridge-tunnel complex.

Assateague Island, a barrier island shared by Virginia and Maryland, is protected in its wild state as a national seashore and wildlife refuge. No buildings except bathhouses and visitor centers are seen along thirty miles (forty-eight kilometers) of the beach. More than 250 species of birds live in or fly through the refuge. Wild ponies have roamed freely here for centuries.

The village of Chincoteague, on Chincoteague Island, is famous for its salt oysters and is the home of three unusual museums—the world's only oyster museum, a waterfowl museum, and the Chincoteague Miniature Pony Farm.

The Community Market
at Lynchburg, southwest
of Charlottesville

PIEDMONT

Many historic points of interest are clustered in the Piedmont. A good place to start is at the visitor center at the south end of Charlottesville. It is also a charming museum, with changing exhibits related to the area. An area in downtown Charlottesville, with a tree-shaded, cobblestone mall, has been designated a historic district. Old buildings here have been preserved and restored.

The University of Virginia, designed by Thomas Jefferson, is nearby. The center of the plan is the Rotunda, a half-size replica of Hadrian's Pantheon in Rome. Rows of academic and dormitory buildings are arranged neatly to the south of the Rotunda. Behind them are landscaped grounds and brick walls that wind in a serpentine line.

A short distance away is Thomas Jefferson's Monticello, one of the most beautiful homes in the nation. Northeast of Monticello, near the town of Orange, is James Madison's home, Montpelier.

Southwest of Charlottesville is Lynchburg, the industrial center of the region. Two historic sites in this vicinity are well worth

Above: The skyline of Richmond, Virginia's capital city
Left: Richmond's Old City Hall

visiting. The first is Appomattox Court House National Historic Park, where General Robert E. Lee's formal surrender to General Ulysses S. Grant brought an end to the Civil War. The second is Red Hill Shrine, just outside the town of Brookneal. This was Patrick Henry's last home. The original house burned in 1919, but an exact reproduction has been constructed.

East of Lynchburg is Virginia's capital city, Richmond, which lies along the fall line. Patrick Henry made his "liberty or death" speech in St. John's Church in Richmond.

Richmond, the capital of Virginia since 1780, was also the capital of the Confederate States of America from 1861 to 1865. The White House of the Confederacy is now a museum; it is close to the state buildings. Richmond is a center of education, light manufacturing, publishing, and transportation.

A spectacular view of
Shenandoah National Park

SHENANDOAH AND THE BLUE RIDGE

The Blue Ridge Mountains, topped by the Skyline Drive and the
Blue Ridge Parkway, run in a southwesterly direction almost
parallel to the state line between Virginia and West Virginia.
Between the parkway and the next range of mountains to the west
lies the wide, beautiful Shenandoah Valley. The Skyline Drive
runs the entire length of Shenandoah National Park.

North of Shenandoah National Park is Winchester, the oldest
colonial city west of the Blue Ridge. It was a major transportation
and supply center during the Civil War.

At several points along and near the Blue Ridge are scenic caves
and caverns, open to the public. Among them are Skyline Caverns
at Front Royal, Luray Caverns in Luray, Shenandoah Caverns at
New Market, and the Caverns of Natural Bridge.

A few miles west of Luray is New Market Battlefield Park. One
of the more unusual battles of the Civil War was fought here. All
of the Confederate troops were young cadets, no more than
twenty years old, from Virginia Military Institute. Each May, some
nine hundred men gather here to reenact that battle.

Natural Bridge (left), a huge natural stone bridge once owned by Thomas Jefferson, lies just a few miles south of Lexington (above).

The restored home in which President Woodrow Wilson was born is in Staunton, a valley town. Lexington was the home of the two greatest Confederate generals, Lee and Jackson. It is also the site of two of Virginia's leading schools—Washington and Lee University and Virginia Military Institute.

Lined by the mountains west of Lexington is Warm Spring Valley. Indians discovered the warm and hot springs flowing in the valley long before Europeans crossed the Blue Ridge. Scotch-Irish settlers came in the early 1700s. A rustic resort was built in Hot Springs in 1766, and there have been hotels and bathhouses there ever since.

A few miles south of Lexington is a huge natural stone bridge. It was surveyed by George Washington and later purchased by Thomas Jefferson. Thirty-four stories underground are the Caverns of Natural Bridge.

The Blue Ridge Parkway runs close by Roanoke, western Virginia's most important city. It is a cultural, medical, industrial, and commercial center for the area.

Twenty miles (thirty-two kilometers) southeast of the city is Booker T. Washington National Monument, a living-history farm.

It is the only unit in the National Park System that interprets life under slavery. Costumed interpreters in the fields and the household work with tools and instruments used at the time Booker T. Washington was a slave.

THE HIGHLANDS

From Roanoke on toward the west and southwest, Virginia's terrain becomes more rugged. The rest of the state is a long, narrow, pointed finger of land that borders on North Carolina, Tennessee, and Kentucky.

A favorite stop on the Blue Ridge Parkway south of Roanoke is Mabry Mill, where several old-time crafts are demonstrated. A water-powered gristmill grinds corn and buckwheat into meal.

A short distance west of the parkway is the town of Galax, which plays host to the Old Fiddlers' Convention each summer.

Up in the mountains west and south of Roanoke is the beautiful college town of Blacksburg. Virginia Polytechnic Institute and State University, founded in 1872, is the state's largest university.

An outdoor historical drama, *The Long Way Home*, is presented throughout the summer in Radford. It tells the story of Mary Draper Ingles, a pioneer woman of the area who was kidnapped by Shawnees and carried off to Ohio in 1755. Some weeks later, she learned that further attacks on Virginia settlers were planned. Determined to warn her friends and family, she escaped and walked all the way back home. It took her seven weeks, but she was reunited with her husband and lived to be eighty-three years old.

Near the Tennessee border is Abingdon, home of the famous Barter Theatre, and on the border is the town of Bristol. Bristol is legally two cities, one in Virginia and one in Tennessee, each with

Mabry Mill, where several crafts are demonstrated and a water-powered gristmill still grinds corn into meal, is a favorite stop on the Blue Ridge Parkway.

its own government and city services, but they share the same main street. From the air, the mountains around Bristol have a rounded look, like loaves of bread that have been patted down by a baker, ready for the oven.

Breaks Interstate Park is shared by Virginia and Kentucky. Here the Big Sandy River plunges through the mountains to create a gorge called the Grand Canyon of the South.

Tourists visit Big Stone Gap in the summer to see presentations of an outdoor drama called *Trail of the Lonesome Pine* or to see the spectacular scenery of the area. Nearby is Natural Tunnel State Park, where there are several stone pinnacles and a giant natural hole in the mountain.

Cumberland Gap is a natural pass in the mountains at the point where Virginia, Tennessee, and Kentucky meet. The pass was used by Daniel Boone and other pioneers as they moved westward for exploration and settlement. There, from spectacular overlooks, visitors can look eastward toward Virginia—the beautiful and cherished land that was ''Mother to Presidents'' and birthplace of a nation.

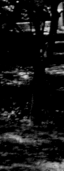

FACTS AT A GLANCE

GENERAL INFORMATION

Statehood: June 25, 1788, tenth state to ratify the Constitution

Origin of Name: Named for Queen Elizabeth I of England, known as the ''Virgin Queen''

State Capital: Richmond, established in 1742

State Nickname: The Old Dominion

State Flag: A white circle on a blue field with a white border contains the state seal. The seal depicts a woman dressed as a warrior, representing Virtue, standing over a conquered body that represents Tyranny. The state motto appears below the figures.

State Motto: *Sic Semper Tyrannis* (Thus Always to Tyrants)

State Bird: Cardinal

State Animal: Foxhound

State Flower: Flowering dogwood

State Tree: Flowering Dogwood

State Song: ''Carry Me Back to Old Virginia,'' by James A. Bland. Bland, a black man who moved to the North prior to the Civil War, wrote the song because he was homesick for Virginia. The wording has caused controversy, however, and the General Assembly is considering substituting another song.

POPULATION

Population: 5,384,709, fourteenth among the states (1980 census)

Population Density: 131 people per sq. mi. (51 people per km²)

Population Distribution: About 71 percent of Virginia's people live in metropolitan areas. The following list shows the state's largest cities:

Norfolk	269,979
Virginia Beach	262,199
Richmond	219,214
Newport News	144,903
Hampton	122,617
Chesapeake	114,486
Portsmouth	104,577
Alexandria	103,217
Roanoke	100,220

(Population figures according to 1980 census)

Population Growth: During the years of the nation's westward expansion, Virginia's population increase was somewhat less than that for the nation as a whole. Between 1930 and 1980, however, the state's population increased by 121 percent, while that for the nation rose by only 85 percent. The trend continued in the 1980s. The list below shows population growth in Virginia since the first census was taken, in 1790.

Year	Population
1790	691,737
1800	807,557
1810	877,683
1820	938,261
1830	1,044,054
1840	1,025,227
1850	1,119,348
1860	1,219,630
1870	1,225,163
1880	1,512,565
1890	1,655,980
1900	1,854,184
1910	2,061,612
1920	2,309,187
1930	2,421,851
1940	2,677,773
1950	3,318,680
1960	3,966,949
1970	4,651,448
1980	5,346,818

GEOGRAPHY

Borders: Virginia's border is very irregular in shape. It is bounded on the east by Chesapeake Bay and the Atlantic Ocean; on the south by North Carolina and Tennessee; and on the west by Kentucky. On the northwest, Virginia is bounded by

Fishermen on Chesapeake Bay

West Virginia. Virginia's northeast border is formed by the Potomac River, which is shared with Maryland. Part of the state—the Delmarva Peninsula and a smattering of islands—is to the east of Chesapeake Bay.

Highest Point: Mount Rogers, in the Blue Ridge Mountains, 5,729 ft. (1,746 m)

Lowest Point: Sea level, along the coast

Greatest Distances: East to west—470 mi. (756 km)
North to south—200 mi. (322 km)

Area: 40,767 sq. mi. (105,587 km²); includes 1,063 sq. mi. (2,753 km²) of inland water

Rank in Area Among the States: Thirty-sixth

Rivers: Four major rivers flow west to east and empty into Chesapeake Bay—the Potomac, Rappahannock, York, and James. These rivers cut Virginia's bay shoreline into three long peninsulas. Other major river systems exit Virginia before they empty into the Atlantic; these include the Chowan and Roanoke river basins. Two river systems in the western region of the state flow east to west and are part of the Mississippi River basin. These are the New River basin and the Tennessee and Big Sandy river basins.

Kerr Reservoir, on the Virginia-North Carolina border, is the largest of the state's many artificially created lakes.

Lakes: Virginia has nine major lakes: John H. Kerr Reservoir, Claytor Lake, John W. Flannagan Reservoir, Lake Anna, Lake Gaston, Leesville Reservoir, Philpott Reservoir, Smith Mountain Lake, and South Holston Lake. Artificially created lakes cover more than 160,000 acres (64,750 hectares). Virginia's largest natural lake is Lake Drummond, in Dismal Swamp, covering 3,200 acres (1,295 hectares).

Topography: Virginia has three distinct land areas: the Atlantic Coastal Plain (also called the Tidewater) in the east; the Piedmont Plateau in the central part of the state; and the mountains of the west and northwest. The Tidewater is a low-lying area sloping gently from the fall line to the sea. A fall line is an imaginary line where rivers descend sharply, through white-water rapids and waterfalls, on their way to the ocean. The triangle-shaped Piedmont varies in width and elevation as it slopes from the base of the Blue Ridge to the fall line in the east. Between the Blue Ridge and the Allegheny Mountains, in the northwest, is the Valley of Virginia, actually six valleys separated by ridges. Part of the state, the southern tip of the Delmarva Peninsula, lies between Chesapeake Bay and the Atlantic Ocean, and there are several offshore islands in the Atlantic.

Climate: The climate of Virginia is generally mild and humid. Temperatures in the mountains of the west tend to be lower than those along the eastern coastal plain. In January, the average temperature in the coastal plain is 41° F. (5° C); in the mountain regions, the average is 32° F. (0° C). In July, the coastal region's average temperature is 78° F. (26° C), while the mountain regions have an average of 68° F.

(20° C). The highest temperature recorded in the state was 110° F. (43° C), at Columbia on July 5, 1900 and at Balcony Falls on July 15, 1954. The record low temperature was -29° F. (-34° C), at Monterey on February 10, 1899. There are four distinct seasons; frost is common in the winter, even at the coast. Precipitation (rain, melted snow, and other moisture) is lightest in northwest Virginia, averaging about 36 in. (91 cm) in the Shenandoah Valley. In the southern part of the state, precipitation averages about 44 in. (112 cm) yearly. Snowfall ranges from 5 to 10 in. (13 to 25 cm) in the coastal regions to 25 to 30 in. (64 to 76 cm) in the western mountains.

NATURE

Trees: Ash, oak, pine, birch, locust, sweet gum, black tupelo, and poplar trees are common in Virginia. The coastal areas abound in pine trees; hardwoods predominate on the inland slopes and ridges.

Wild Plants: Various wildflowers enhance the beauty of Virginia's mountains during their seasons, particularly trailing arbutus, mountain laurel, azaleas, and rhododendrons. In the Great Dismal Swamp, there are huge numbers of such rare wildflowers as dwarf trillium and silky camellia.

Animals: White-tailed deer, elk, black bears, bobcats, foxes, raccoons, opossums, nutria, skunks, squirrels, rabbits, beavers, mink, river otters; wild ponies live on Assateague Island

Birds: Pileated woodpeckers, prothonotary warblers, wood ducks, orchard and northern orioles, scarlet and summer tanagers, grosbeaks, hummingbirds, wrens, peewees, thrushes, swifts, ruffed grouse, wild turkeys, quail, mourning doves, woodcocks, terns, ibises

Fish: Bass, bream, bluegill, carp, catfish, crappie, perch, and sunfish in freshwater ponds and streams; croakers, hogfish, flounders, menhaden, sea bass, striped bass, and sea trout in the tidal waters; clams, crabs, oysters, and scallops in Chesapeake Bay and shallow coastal waters

GOVERNMENT

The government of Virginia consists of three branches: the legislative, executive, and judicial.

The legislative branch is called the General Assembly. There are two houses, the senate, with 40 members, and the house of delegates, with 100 members. Boundaries of the legislative districts are determined on the basis of population. The responsibilities of the General Assembly include making laws, setting state taxes, and approving expenditures of state money.

Three officials of the executive branch—the governor, lieutenant governor, and attorney general—are elected. Other state officials are appointed by the governor and confirmed by both houses of the General Assembly. Governors are elected for a four-year term and are not permitted to succeed themselves. The responsibilities of the governor include enforcing the laws and preparing the state budget. The governor is commander-in-chief of the state police and the Virginia militia.

The judicial branch interprets laws and tries cases. Virginia's supreme court consists of a chief justice and six other justices, each of whom is elected to a twelve-year term. The court of appeals has nine justices, who serve eight-year terms. Lower courts are the thirty-one circuit courts, district courts, and juvenile and domestic-relations courts.

Number of Counties: 95, plus 41 independent cities

U.S. Representatives: 10

Electoral Votes: 12

Voting Qualifications: Eighteen years of age and must have been registered in the precinct of residence at least thirty-one days before the election

EDUCATION

The first free schools in the United States were established in Virginia. The Syms Free School in Hampton was founded in 1634 and the Eaton Free School, also in Hampton, began accepting students about 1640. The statewide public school system began in 1870. By state law, children aged six to sixteen are required to attend school.

Nearly 980,000 students attend Virginia's 1,757 schools in 140 school divisions. The state board of education is committed to the improvement of public schools and can point to a number of statistics that indicate considerable success. The dropout rate for high school students declined from 5.7 percent in 1979 to 4.4 percent in 1985, and 64 percent of graduates were going on to further education as compared with 53 percent ten years earlier. Virginia places seventh among the twenty-two states that use national tests. Average test scores earned by Virginia students are above the national average.

Vocational education programs serve 345,000 secondary students and 157,000 adults.

There are fourteen state-supported four-year colleges and universities in Virginia, as well as twenty-three community colleges, located on thirty-three campuses. The largest state-supported schools are Virginia Polytechnic Institute and State University, in Blacksburg; Virginia Commonwealth University, in Richmond; Old Dominion University, in Norfolk; the University of Virginia, in Charlottesville; George Mason University, in Fairfax; and the College of William and Mary, with campuses in Williamsburg and Newport News. The College of William and Mary, founded in 1693 at Williamsburg, is the second-oldest institution of higher learning in the United States. There are about twenty-four private four-year institutions in the state.

Wheat and apples are among the principal products produced in Virginia.

ECONOMY AND INDUSTRY

Principal Products:
Agriculture: Tobacco, peanuts, sweet potatoes, apples, peaches, hay, soybeans, corn, wheat, milk, beef cattle, chickens, turkeys
Manufacturing: Food and food products, lumber and wood products, tobacco products, chemical and allied products, electric and electronic equipment, transportation equipment, textiles, apparel, paper and allied products, fabricated metal products
Fishing: Menhaden, clams, crabs, oysters
Natural Resources: Virginia's forests cover nearly 60 percent of the total land area. The principal minerals found in the state are coal, kyanite (used in ceramics and refractory products), quartzite, soapstone, limestone, sandstone, sand and gravel

Business and Trade: Virginia ranks twentieth among the fifty states in wholesale trade and eleventh in retail trade. The major retail market area is Fairfax County, which is part of the Washington, D.C., metropolitan area. Billions of dollars worth of imports and exports pass through the Hampton Roads estuary at the mouth of the James River each year. Coal is a leading export product and oil the principal import.

Communication: The *Virginia Gazette*, founded in 1736, was Virginia's first newspaper. The *Alexandria Gazette*, founded in 1784, is one of the country's oldest continuously published dailies. Among the 139 newspapers published in Virginia today, 36 are dailies; 325 other periodicals are also published in the state. The newspapers with the largest circulation are the Norfolk *Virginia Pilot*, the *Richmond News Leader*, the Roanoke *Times & World News*, and the *Richmond Times-Dispatch*. There are 251 radio stations and 48 television stations in the state.

Transportation: The Little River Turnpike, built in the 1780s, was the nation's first toll road. Today, Virginia's network of state-maintained highways is the third largest in the nation. Six interstate routes cross the state—I-77, I-79, I-81, I-95, I-64, and I-66. Important segments of the state's ground transportation system are the several bridge-tunnels in the Hampton Roads area. The Chesapeake Bay Bridge-Tunnel is 23 mi. (37 km) long; it connects the mainland with the Eastern Shore.

Rail freight service is provided by thirteen railroads and includes more than 4,000 mi. (6,437 km) of track. Major north-south rail lines meet major lines that run east and west across the state.

Passenger rail service is provided by Amtrak, with eight trains making scheduled stops in the state. Amtrak also operates an auto-train (a ferry service for privately owned cars and their passengers) between Lorton, Virginia, and Sanford, Florida. Metro provides metropolitan transit service between several northern Virginia municipalities and Washington, D.C.

There are twelve airports in Virginia and two more just across the state line (in Bluefield, West Virginia, and Bristol, Tennessee) that provide scheduled commercial airline service. Northern Virginia is served by the three airports in the Washington metropolitan area: Dulles International, near Chantilly; Manassas Municipal, at Manassas; and Washington National, in Arlington. In addition, there are sixty-seven general aviation airports licensed for public use.

Millions of tons of cargo for foreign trade are moved through Virginia's port area. A fine harbor, called Hampton Roads, lies between the mouth of the James River and Chesapeake Bay. Marine terminals at four cities—Newport News, Norfolk, Portsmouth, and Chesapeake—serve the area. Other transportation systems interconnect with the Hampton Roads area, including 5 railroads, 10 airlines, and approximately 135 motor freight carriers. The area is a leader in foreign-trade tonnage.

SOCIAL AND CULTURAL LIFE

Museums: The more than two hundred museums within Virginia range from those with large fine arts collections to historic house museums. The Virginia Museum of Fine Arts, in Richmond, was the first state-supported art museum in the United States. Also in Richmond are the Science Museum of Virginia and several house museums. Norfolk's Chrysler Museum is noted for its glassware collection. The Mariners' Museum in Newport News has a fine maritime museum; boats, models, paintings, and artifacts related to worldwide maritime history and shipping are on display.

Virginia has more historic sites maintained and open to the public than any other state. Some of the best known and most popular are George Washington's home, Mount Vernon; Thomas Jefferson's home, Monticello; and the entire village of Colonial Williamsburg.

Hampton University, one of the earliest institutions in the South founded to provide higher education for students of all races, has an outstanding collection of African and Native American artifacts.

Libraries: Virginia's first public library was established in 1794 at Alexandria. Today, nearly one hundred county, city, town, and regional libraries serve the people of Virginia. The Virginia State Library and Archives, in Richmond, is a large research library. This library, as well as the libraries of the University of Virginia in Charlottesville and the College of William and Mary in Williamsburg, have collections of personal papers of many of the outstanding citizens of the state, such as Washington, Jefferson, Madison, and Lee.

Performing Arts: Virginia has a number of theaters with an international reputation. Wolf Trap Farm Park for the Performing Arts, in Vienna (near Washington, D.C.), is maintained and managed by the National Park Service, the first such park in the nation. Performers from all over the world have been featured here in opera, jazz, modern dance, ballet, and symphony concerts. Filene Center, the Wolf Trap theater and concert hall, burned in 1982 but was quickly rebuilt.

The Barter Theatre, in Abingdon, is state-supported. Founded during the Great Depression of the 1930s, it got its name from the practice of allowing farmers in the area to barter their farm produce for admission tickets. Richmond and Norfolk are important centers for theatrical and musical performances. An annual Shakespeare Festival is presented in Williamsburg.

Sports and Recreation: Virginia's single major-league sports team is the Washington Redskins football team, headquartered near Dulles International Airport. Two baseball farm teams are based in Norfolk and Richmond.

Virginia's most popular sport is collegiate basketball. Divisional championships have been won in recent years by the University of Virginia, Virginia Union University, Old Dominion, and Virginia Commonwealth University. Old Dominion's Lady Monarchs have won the national tournament of the Association for Intercollegiate Athletics for Women.

Tennis, golf, and water sports are popular in Virginia. The state has twenty-five state parks, a national park, two national forests, and four scenic parkways. Shenandoah National Park is one of the nation's most visited national parks. Thousands of miles of hiking trails, some 1,500 mi. (2,414 km) of well-stocked streams, and marvelous shorelines along Chesapeake Bay and the Atlantic Ocean attract vacationers.

Historic Sites and Landmarks:

Appomattox Court House National Historic Park, near the village of Appomattox, is a restored village of twenty-seven buildings that includes the site of the surrender of General Robert E. Lee to General Ulysses S. Grant, which ended the Civil War.

Appomattox Manor, in Hopewell, a home built about 1763, was used by some of General Ulysses S. Grant's staff during the last year of the war. A cabin was built on the grounds to serve as Grant's headquarters, and President Lincoln visited him here on official business.

James Monroe's law office in Fredericksburg is a museum containing such items as the desk on which the Monroe Doctrine was signed.

Arlington National Cemetery, in Arlington, contains the graves of many famous Americans, both civilian and military. Within the grounds are *Arlington House*, the home of Robert E. Lee from 1831 to 1861; the *Tomb of the Unknowns*; a *Memorial Amphitheater* used for various ceremonies; and the graves of presidents William Howard Taft and John F. Kennedy.

Ash Lawn, in Charlottesville, was the home of President James Monroe. The modest house, on a beautiful estate, is set on a hilltop near the home of Monroe's friend Thomas Jefferson.

Bacon's Castle, on the James River, built in 1665, is one of the oldest brick houses in English America. It was the stronghold of a group of rebels led by Nathaniel Bacon, who rose up against the rule of the colonial governor in 1676.

Berkeley Plantation, in Charles City, on the James River, was the birthplace of William Henry Harrison, a signer of the Declaration of Independence and later ninth president of the United States. Settlers celebrated the first Thanksgiving Day here in 1619. The familiar tune "Taps" was written here during the Civil War.

Booker T. Washington National Monument, near Burnt Chimney, southeast of Roanoke, is the only part of the National Park System that demonstrates life under slavery. It is a living-history farm.

Carter's Grove Plantation, in Williamsburg, was founded by one of colonial Virginia's wealthiest planters. The plantation is now owned and maintained by Colonial Williamsburg.

Colonial Williamsburg, in Williamsburg, was the capital of colonial Virginia. More than five hundred buildings comprise what has been described as the most elaborately restored and rebuilt living-history museum in the world. Costumed interpreters re-create eighteenth-century life in the village and artisans demonstrate traditional crafts.

Edgar Allan Poe Museum, in Richmond, occupies five buildings and enclosed gardens, and displays many items related to the life of the poet and author. One structure, the Old Stone House, is the oldest building (c. 1750) within the original boundaries of Richmond. Especially interesting is a scale model of the city as it looked during Poe's lifetime.

George Washington Birthplace National Monument, in Westmoreland County, is a reconstruction of the colonial farm on which the first president was born.

George Washington Grist Mill, on Mount Vernon Memorial Highway near Alexandria, is a reconstruction of the original mill owned and operated by George Washington over a period of nearly thirty years.

Gunston Hall, a short distance down the Potomac River from Mount Vernon, was built in 1755 by George Mason, known as the Father of the Bill of Rights.

Harpers Ferry National Historical Park covers land in three states—Virginia, West Virginia, and Maryland—at the junction of the Shenandoah and Potomac rivers. This is where John Brown led a small group of abolitionists in an unsuccessful raid on an arsenal in 1859. Their aim was to arm some runaway slaves and help them establish a free state in the mountains.

James Monroe Law and Memorial Library, in Fredericksburg, is a museum of items used by the fifth president, housed in his former office.

Jamestown and Jamestown Festival Park, in Jamestown, mark the site of the first permanent English settlement in the New World. At Jamestown Festival Park, costumed interpreters demonstrate what life was like for the early settlers. Full-sized replicas of the three ships that brought the colonists from England are moored in the harbor; there are reconstructions of the original fort and of an Indian village.

Michie Tavern, in Charlottesville, is a complex of pre-Revolutionary buildings—tavern, kitchen, smokehouse, gristmill, and springhouse. The tavern now houses a restaurant that features dishes of the colonial era.

Monticello, in Charlottesville, is the mountaintop home of Thomas Jefferson, the third president. He designed the thirty-five-room house and supervised its construction over a forty-year period.

Montpelier, near Orange, was the home of the nation's fourth president, James Madison. It was recently acquired by the National Trust for Historic Preservation and opened to the public.

Mount Vernon, on the Potomac River near Alexandria, is the home of George Washington. George Washington inherited the property from his half-brother Lawrence in 1752; building was completed in 1787. This is one of the most popular historic shrines in the United States.

Museum of American Frontier Culture, in Staunton, is one of the state's newest museums. Four farms make up the outdoor living-history museum. Three of the farms depict farms typical of the European homelands of Virginia's early settlers—Great Britain, Northern Ireland, and Germany. The fourth farm reproduces life in the pioneer days of the Shenandoah Valley.

New Market Battlefield Park, in New Market, has a museum with exhibits covering the entire history of the Civil War. A restored nineteenth-century farm is on the premises.

St. John's Church, in Richmond, was the site, in 1775, of the Second Virginia Convention. It was to that assembly that Patrick Henry made his "Give Me Liberty or Give Me Death!" speech.

Shirley Plantation, on the James River between Richmond and Williamsburg, has been the home of nine generations of the Carter family. It has a complete set of eighteenth-century buildings.

Stonewall Jackson House, in Lexington, was the home of the famous Confederate general. Some of his furniture and personal belongings are on display.

Stonewall Jackson's Headquarters, in Winchester, is the house in which General Jackson planned his Shenandoah Valley campaign. The office looks much the way it did when he was in residence, and many Jackson items are on display.

War Memorial Museum of Virginia, in Newport News, has more than thirty thousand artifacts that trace U.S. military history from the time of the American Revolution to the present.

White House of the Confederacy, in Richmond, was the home of Confederate President Jefferson Davis from 1861 to 1865. The Museum of the Confederacy is next door.

Woodrow Wilson's Birthplace, in Staunton, is a large Greek Revival house built in 1846. Wilson, the twenty-eighth president of the United States, was born there in 1856. Furnishings that belonged to the Wilson family and a collection of Wilson items are displayed.

Yorktown, part of Colonial National Historical Park, was the site of the final battle of the American Revolution.

Assateague Island National Seashore is protected as a natural wilderness.

Other Interesting Places to Visit:

Assateague Island National Seashore, a barrier island partly in Virginia, partly in Maryland, is the largest undeveloped expanse of seashore between Massachusetts and North Carolina, and is protected as a natural wilderness by the National Park Service. Each summer, some of the island's wild horses, called Chincoteague ponies, are rounded up for sale. Wild Pony Roundup Day is celebrated with carnivals, shows, and picnics.

Blue Ridge Parkway is a highway through western Virginia and North Carolina. There are no commercial establishments or residences on the parkway, said to be the longest scenic drive in the world.

Breaks Interstate Park, at Breaks, is on the border of Virginia and Kentucky and is managed cooperatively by the two states. It is on the rim of the largest river canyon east of the Mississippi River.

Busch Gardens-The Old Country, in Williamsburg, is a beautiful landscaped entertainment park. Several European "villages" depict the countries from which early settlers came to the Tidewater area of Virginia.

Chesapeake Bay Bridge-Tunnel is a 23-mile (37-kilometer) link between the Virginia Beach-Norfolk area and the Eastern Shore.

Chincoteague Miniature Pony Farm, in Chincoteague. Famous throughout the world are the miniature Chincoteague ponies that roam wild on the marshy island.

Chrysler Museum, in Norfolk, has an outstanding collection of glass and other arts, representing many periods that cover nearly five thousand years. It is rated among the top museums in the United States.

Great Dismal Swamp National Wildlife Refuge, near Suffolk, covers more than 102,000 acres (41,278 hectares) of water and forested land. Boat and canoe tours into the heart of the swamp are available.

Luray Caverns, in Luray, contain huge underground rooms with colorful rock formations. An organ has been installed in one of the rooms and music reverberates off the stalactites. An extensive collection of antique cars, carriages, and coaches is on the premises as well.

Mariners Museum, in Newport News, is a grand collection of miniature ships, figureheads, and other items of maritime and shipping history.

Mattaponi Indian Museum, in West Point, offers classes in Indian arts and crafts, herbs, medicine, and dance.

NASA Langley Visitor Center, in Hampton, has exhibits related to aeronautics and space exploration. Among the displays are a moon rock, the Apollo Command Module, and a space suit worn on the moon.

Natural Bridge of Virginia, in Natural Bridge, is a bridge 215 feet (66 meters) high considered to be one of the natural wonders of the world. A highway runs across the top.

Natural Chimneys, near Mount Solon, are seven limestone towers that rise 120 feet (37 meters) above the floor of the Shenandoah Valley.

Norfolk Botanical Gardens, in Norfolk, has flowering plants in bloom year-round. Visitors can walk, or ride on trams or canal boats.

Peaks of Otter, near Bedford, is one of the most popular stops along the Blue Ridge Parkway. People have been coming to enjoy the mountain views since Thomas Jefferson's day.

Richmond Children's Museum, in Richmond, is a "hands-on" museum designed for the delight of children two to twelve years old.

Shenandoah Caverns, near Shenandoah, is another group of colorful caves.

Shenandoah National Park, near Luray, is a long, narrow parkland running north and south through the Blue Ridge Mountains on either side of Skyline Drive. At many points along the highway, there are wide vistas revealing the green farmlands of the Shenandoah Valley and the Valley of Virginia, far below.

Skyline Caverns, near Front Royal, are known for their rare, flowerlike rock formations of calcite.

State Capitol, in Richmond. Thomas Jefferson chose the design for this historic legislative building, modeled after an ancient Roman temple. Richmond's Capitol Square includes the governor's Executive Mansion, the oldest state executive's residence in the nation.

"The Long Way Home," presented throughout the summer in Radford, is a historic drama that tells the story of a heroic pioneer woman who survived an Indian attack in 1756.

"Trail of the Lonsome Pine," presented during July and August in Big Stone Gap, is a musical drama about the boom of coal mining in Virginia and the changes the discovery of coal brought to mountain life.

University of Virginia, in Charlottesville, was founded by Thomas Jefferson, who considered this the most important achievement of his life. He designed the original buildings and the famous serpentine brick wall.

Virginia Museum of Transportation, in Roanoke, has the largest collection of railroad memorabilia in the South.

IMPORTANT DATES

3,000 B.C. — Woodland Indians inhabit areas around Chesapeake Bay

A.D. 1492 — Columbus reaches America

1607 — Colonists arrive and establish Jamestown as the first settlement of Virginia Colony

1614 — John Rolfe exports cultivated tobacco

1619 — First women and first blacks arrive in Jamestown; first meeting of the Virginia House of Burgesses is convened

1649 — Slavery is made permanent in Virginia

1676 — Bacon's Rebellion

1693 — The College of William and Mary is chartered

1699 — Williamsburg (then called Middle Plantation) becomes the capital of Virginia

1749 — Liberty Hall Academy is founded, forerunner of Washington and Lee University

1765—Patrick Henry speaks against the Stamp Act

1775—Revolutionary War begins

1776—Declaration of Independence, written by Thomas Jefferson, is adopted by the Continental Congress; Virginia adopts its first constitution

1786—The Virginia Statute of Religious Freedom is adopted

1787—U.S. Constitution is written and adopted in Philadelphia; James Madison earns the title of Father of the Constitution because of his work in writing and arguing for it

1788—Virginia joins the Union

1789—George Washington becomes the first president of the United States

1800—Slave named Gabriel leads a revolt

1801—Thomas Jefferson becomes the third president of the United States

1809—James Madison becomes the fourth president of the United States

1817—James Monroe becomes the fifth president of the United States

1825—The University of Virginia opens

1831—Nat Turner leads a slave revolt

1833—The first steam-driven railroad is built in Virginia

1841—William Henry Harrison becomes the ninth president of the United States; dies in office the same year; John Tyler becomes the tenth president

1849—Zachary Taylor becomes the twelfth president of the United States

1859—John Brown leads a raid on the U.S. arsenal at Harpers Ferry

1860—Abraham Lincoln is elected sixteenth president of the United States

1861—Virginia secedes from the Union; Confederate States of America is formed; the Civil War begins

1862—*Monitor* and *Merrimac* battle in Hampton Roads, the first battle of ironclad ships; Confederate forces win the Second Battle of Bull Run

1863—Confederate forces are victorious at Chancellorsville

1864—Lincoln is reelected; Richmond falls to the Union army

1865 — Confederate General Robert E. Lee surrenders to Union General Ulysses S. Grant at Appomattox Court House; Civil War ends

1870 — Virginia is readmitted to the Union

1882 — The General Assembly abolishes the poll tax

1883 — The first carload of coal is hauled to Norfolk by the Norfolk and Western Railroad

1891 — Railroad line reaches Big Stone Gap

1900 — Outbreak of yellow fever in Hampton; Virginia-born army doctor Walter Reed heads research work that results in eradication of the disease

1901-02 — The Virginia Constitutional Convention meets

1904 — The poll tax law is reestablished

1908 — The Virginia Child Labor Law is passed

1909 — The Virginia Equal Suffrage League is formed

1913 — Woodrow Wilson becomes the twenty-eighth president of the United States

1914-18 — World War I

1918 — First women are admitted to a state college (the College of William and Mary)

1920 — Women gain suffrage through the Nineteenth Amendment

1921 — Two women are elected to the Virginia General Assembly

1926 — Harry F. Byrd becomes governor of Virginia; Richard E. Byrd and Floyd Bennett fly over the North Pole

1928 — Antilynching law is passed

1931 — Harry F. Byrd becomes a U.S. senator

1933 — Barter Theatre gives its first performance

1935 — Virginia Museum of Fine Arts, the first state art museum in the country, is completed

1939 — World War II begins in Europe

1941 — The United States enters the war

1945 — World War II ends

1954 — *Brown v. Board of Education of Topeka* case marks the beginning of attempts at racial integration of southern schools

1959 — The Virginia Supreme Court of Appeals outlaws school closing; school integration begins

1964 — The Civil Rights Act of 1964 is passed; the Chesapeake Bay Bridge-Tunnel opens

1971 — The present-day Virginia constitution is adopted; the U.S. Supreme Court approves court-ordered busing

1976 — Lawrence A. Davies and Noel C. Taylor are elected the first black mayors of Virginia cities

1988 — Virginia celebrates bicentennial of statehood

1989 — L. Douglas Wilder is elected the first black governor of Virginia, becoming the first black governor in United States history since Reconstruction

ARTHUR ASHE

PEARL BAILEY

IMPORTANT PEOPLE

Samuel Chapman Armstrong (1839-1893), educator; agent of Freedmen's Bureau; founder and first principal of Hampton Normal and Industrial Institute

Arthur Ashe (1943-   ), born in Richmond; professional tennis player, television sports commentator, coach; winner of the 1975 Wimbledon and 1968-70 Davis Cup tournaments

Pearl Bailey (1918-   ), born in Newport News; singer, recording artist, actress, author; famed for her roles on stage in *Hello, Dolly* and in the movie *Porgy and Bess*

Warren Beatty (1938-   ), born in Richmond; actor, director, producer; directed and acted in *Heaven Can Wait* (1978); produced, directed, acted in, and won the 1981 Academy Award for best director for *Reds*

John Blair (1732-1800), born in Williamsburg; jurist; delegate to the Constitutional Convention of 1787; associate justice of the U.S. Supreme Court (1789-96); first president of the College of William and Mary

Carter Braxton (1736-1797), born in Newington; Revolutionary War patriot; member of the Virginia House of Burgesses; delegate to the Continental Congress; signer of the Declaration of Independence

Harry Flood Byrd (1887-1966), born in Winchester; politician; governor (1926-30); U.S. senator (1933-65)

Richard Evelyn Byrd (1888-1957), born in Winchester; naval aviator, navigator, explorer; brother of U.S. Senator Harry F. Byrd; Arctic and Antarctic explorer; first person, along with Floyd Bennett, to fly to the North Pole (1926)

William Byrd II (1674-1744), born on a James River plantation; planter, author, diarist; founded the city of Richmond

RICHARD E. BYRD

James Branch Cabell (1879-1958), born in Richmond; novelist, essayist, newspaper columnist; best known for his controversial romance novel *Jurgen*

Alvin Pleasant (A.P.) Carter (1891-1960), born in Maces Spring; musician; formed the Carter Family singers; the group recorded more than three hundred mountain, folk, and country music songs (1927-43)

George Rogers Clark (1752-1818), born near Charlottesville; Revolutionary War soldier; won important victories in the Northwest Territory that gave the United States claim to the areas west to the Mississippi River and north to the Great Lakes

GEORGE ROGERS CLARK

William Clark (1770-1838), born in Caroline County; frontiersman, explorer; younger brother of George Rogers Clark; leader with Meriwether Lewis of an expedition to explore the Louisiana Territory; explored the Yellowstone River

Virginius Dabney (1901-   ), born in University; editor, historian, author; editor of the *Richmond Times-Dispatch* (1936-69); received the 1947 Pulitzer Prize in editorial writing; author of numerous books on Virginia history; president of the Virginia Historical Society (1969-72)

Moses Jacob Ezekiel (1844-1917), born in Richmond; sculptor; studied art at the Royal Academy in Berlin; knighted by both Germany and Italy for his work; created the monument to the Confederate dead in Arlington National Cemetery

ELLA FITZGERALD

Ella Fitzgerald (1918-   ), born in Newport News; jazz singer and entertainer; winner of eight Grammy awards; recipient of the prestigious American Music Award (1978); recipient of Kennedy Center Honors award (1979)

Douglas Southall Freeman (1886-1953), born in Lynchburg; editor, historian, author; received Pulitzer Prizes in biography for *R.E. Lee* (1935) and *George Washington*, vols. 1-6 (1958, posthumously)

Ellen Glasgow (1874-1945), born in Richmond; novelist; author of books about Virginia society and history; received the 1942 Pulitzer Prize in fiction for *In This Our Life*

Freeman Fisher Gosden (1899-1982), born in Richmond; radio comedian; famous for his role as Amos in the popular radio comedy "Amos and Andy"

ELLEN GLASGOW

WM. HENRY HARRISON

STONEWALL JACKSON

JOHN PAUL JONES

LIGHTHORSE HARRY LEE

Earl Henry Hamner, Jr. (1923-   ), born in Schuyler; author, producer; creator of two long-running television series, "The Waltons" and "Falcon Crest"; received an Emmy for his Christmas special, "The Homecoming" (1974)

William Henry Harrison (1773-1841), born in Charles City County; ninth president of the United States (1841); died after only one month in office

Patrick Henry (1736-1799), born in Hanover County; Revolutionary War patriot; member of the Virginia House of Burgesses (1765); delegate to the First and Second Continental congresses; governor of the Commonwealth of Virginia (1776-79, 1784-86); leader in the movement to add the first ten amendments (the Bill of Rights) to the U.S. Constitution

Thomas Jonathan "Stonewall" Jackson (1824-1863), born in Clarksburg; professional soldier; graduate of the U.S. Military Academy; one of the best and most famous of the Confederate generals; died of a battle wound

Thomas Jefferson (1743-1826), born in Goochland, now Albemarle County; third president of the United States (1801-09); lawyer, statesman, political theorist, musician, planter, architect, archaeologist; facilitated expansion of the nation to the West through the Louisiana Purchase and the Lewis and Clark Expedition; founder of the University of Virginia

John Paul Jones (1747-1792), born in Scotland, settled in Fredericksburg (1773); naval officer; commanded the ship *Bonhomme Richard* during a 1779 battle with the British in which he became famous for replying to a British demand for surrender, "I have not yet begun to fight"

Francis Lightfoot Lee (1734-1797), born in Westmoreland County; politician; member of the Virginia House of Burgesses (1758-76); signer of the Declaration of Independence; delegate to the First Continental Congress

Henry "Lighthorse Harry" Lee (1756-1818), born in Prince William County; soldier and statesman; father of Confederate General Robert E. Lee; captain of Virginia cavalry in the Revolutionary War; governor of Virginia (1792-95); U.S. representative (1799-1801); author of the famous epitaph of George Washington, "First in war, first in peace, and first in the hearts of his countrymen"

Richard Henry Lee (1732-1794), born in Westmoreland County; Revolutionary War patriot; brother of Francis Lightfoot Lee; delegate to the Continental Congress (1774-79), where he introduced a resolution that led to the Declaration of Independence; signer of the Declaration of Independence; delegate to the Continental Congress (1784-89); president of the Congress (1784-85); U.S. senator (1789-92); enthusiastic supporter of the Bill of Rights

Robert E. Lee (1807-1870), born in Westmoreland County; Civil War general; commander of the Confederate army; his surrender to Union General Ulysses S. Grant on April 9, 1865, signaled the end of the Civil War; president of Washington College (1865-70), now called Washington and Lee University

Meriwether Lewis (1774-1809), born in Albemarle County; explorer; named by President Thomas Jefferson to lead an expedition, along with William Clark, to explore the lands of the Louisiana Purchase and document a land route from the Mississippi River to the Pacific Ocean; governor of the Louisiana Territory (1807-09)

Shirley MacLaine (1934-   ), born in Richmond; actress, dancer, author; won the 1983 Academy Award for best actress in the film *Terms of Endearment*; author of several autobiographical books

SHIRLEY MacLAINE

James Madison (1751-1836), born in Port Conway; fourth president of the United States (1809-17); member of committee that drafted Virginia's constitution (1776); delegate to the Constitutional Convention, where his role in drafting the document earned him the title "Father of the Constitution"; one of the authors of *The Federalist* letters; largely responsible for drafting the Bill of Rights; U.S. secretary of state (1801-09)

JAMES MADISON

Alf Johnson Mapp, Jr. (1925-   ), born in Portsmouth; educator, historian, author; editorial writer for *Virginia Pilot*, Norfolk (1954-58); professor of English, journalism, and history at Old Dominion University (1961-   ); received Outstanding American Educator award (1972)

George Catlett Marshall (1880-1959), born in Uniontown; soldier and statesman; chief of staff of the U.S. Army (1939-45); secretary of state (1947-49); secretary of defense (1950-51); author of the European Recovery Plan, popularly called the Marshall Plan, to rebuild Europe after the war; awarded the 1953 Nobel Peace Prize

John Marshall (1755-1835), born near Germantown, now Midland; jurist; served in the Continental army during the Revolutionary War; member of Virginia executive council (1782-95); member of House of Burgesses (1782-88); U.S. Representative (1799-1800); chief justice of U.S. Supreme Court (1801-35); credited with building the Supreme Court into a strong and equal branch of the federal government

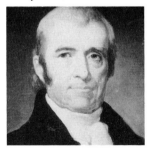

JOHN MARSHALL

Matthew Fontaine Maury (1806-1873), born near Fredericksburg; naval officer, oceanographer; circumnavigated the globe (1826-30); wrote the first textbook on modern oceanography (1855), as well as many books on physical geography

Cyrus Hall McCormick (1809-1884), born in Rockbridge County; inventor, manufacturer, industrialist; invented a reaping machine (1831) that revolutionized agriculture; founder of the International Harvester Company (now called Navistar)

CYRUS McCORMICK

WILLIAM H. McGUFFEY

EDGAR ALLAN POE

WALTER REED

KATE SMITH

William Holmes McGuffey (1800-1873), educator, author; professor at the University of Virginia (1845-73); best known for his *Eclectic Readers*, a series of illustrated readers used in the majority of American schools for many years

James Monroe (1758-1831), born in Westmoreland County; fifth president of the United States (1817-25); lawyer, statesman; member of the Continental Congress (1783-86); U.S. senator (1790-94); U.S. minister to France (1794-96); governor of Virginia (1799-1802); U.S. secretary of state (1811-17); U.S. secretary of war (1814-15); author of the Monroe Doctrine

Edgar Allan Poe (1809-1849), raised in Richmond; distinguished poet, short-story writer, literary critic; credited with originating the modern detective story

Lewis F. Powell (1907-   ), born in Suffolk; jurist; associate justice of the U.S. Supreme Court (1971-87)

Edmund Jennings Randolph (1753-1813), born in Williamsburg; member of the Continental Congress (1779-82); governor of Virginia (1786-88); delegate to the Constitutional Convention (1787); U.S. attorney general (1789-94); U.S. secretary of state (1794-95)

Peyton Randolph (1721-1775), born in Williamsburg; first president of the Continental Congress

Walter Reed (1851-1902), born in Belroi; surgeon; U.S. Army medical officer; discovered how typhoid and yellow fever were spread and thus helped control the diseases

Bill ''Bojangles'' Robinson (1878-1949), born in Richmond; dancer, actor; danced in Broadway musicals and acted and danced in films; famous for his dance scene with Shirley Temple in the film *The Little Colonel*

Winfield Scott (1786-1866), born near Petersburg; army officer; hero of the War of 1812 and expert military strategist; general-in-chief of the U.S. Army (1841-61)

Captain John Smith (1580?-1631), English adventurer, explorer, mapmaker; president of the Jamestown Colony; author of *A Description of New England* and other accounts of his travels

Kathryn Elizabeth (Kate) Smith (1909-1986), born in Greenville; singer, actress; known as the ''first lady of radio'' during the 1940s; inspired the wartime nation and became a symbol of American patriotism for her singing of ''God Bless America''

Sam Snead (1912-   ), born in Hot Springs; professional golfer, author; winner of more than a hundred tournaments, including the PGA Championship, Masters Golf Tournament, and the British Open; elected to the PGA Hall of Fame (1963); author of many self-help golf books

James Ewell Brown (Jeb) Stuart (1833-1864), born in Patrick County; Confederate army cavalry officer (1861-64)

Zachary Taylor (1784-1850), born in Orange County; twelfth president of the United States (1849-50); fought in several military campaigns

John Tyler (1790-1862), born in Charles City County; tenth president of the United States (1841-45); governor of Virginia (1825-27); U.S. senator (1827-36); vice-president (1841); became president when William Henry Harrison died in office one month after inauguration

Edward Virginius Valentine (1838-1930), born in Richmond; sculptor; works include the likenesses of Thomas Jefferson and General Thomas "Stonewall" Jackson

S. S. Van Dine, pen name of Willard Huntington Wright (1888-1939), author, critic; best known for his detective stories featuring the fictional hero Philo Vance

Booker T. Washington (1856-1915), born a slave in Franklin County; educator, public speaker, author; organizer and president of Tuskegee Institute in Alabama, founded primarily for the education of black students

George Washington (1732-1799), born in Westmoreland County; first president of the United States (1789-97); member of the House of Burgesses (1759-74); delegate to Continental Congresses (1774-83); president of the Constitutional Convention (1787); unanimously elected first president of the United States

Woodrow Wilson (1856-1924), born in Staunton; twenty-eighth president of the United States (1913-21); scholar, educator, statesman; president of Princeton University (1902-10); governor of New Jersey (1911-13); as president, he led the country through the days of World War I; at Paris Peace Conference, he assured the acceptance of the League of Nations pact; was awarded the 1919 Nobel Peace Prize

Thomas Kennerly (Tom) Wolfe, Jr. (1931-   ), born in Richmond; journalist, author; known for sharp, incisive style; books include *The Right Stuff* (1979) and *From Bauhaus to Our House* (1981)

Carter Godwin Woodson (1875-1950), born in New Canton; historian, author; dean, Howard University (1919-20); dean, West Virginia State College (1920-22); founded Associated Publishers, Inc. (1922) to publish works on black culture; wrote many books on black history; was awarded the Spingarn Medal (1926)

George Wythe (1726-1806), born in Elizabeth City County; lawyer, judge; wrote the original Virginia protest against the Stamp Act; delegate to the Continental Congress (1775-77); signer of the Declaration of Independence; first professor of law in the U.S., at the College of William and Mary (1779-89)

JEB STUART

ZACHARY TAYLOR

BOOKER T. WASHINGTON

WOODROW WILSON

GOVERNORS

Patrick Henry	1776-1779	Henry Alexander Wise	1856-1860
Thomas Jefferson	1779-1781	John Letcher	1860-1864
William Fleming	1781	William Smith	1864-1865
Thomas Nelson, Jr.	1781	Francis Harrison Pierpont	1865-1868
David Jameson	1781	Henry Horatio Wells	1868-1869
Benjamin Harrison	1781-1784	Gilbert Carlton Walker	1869-1874
Patrick Henry	1784-1786	James Lawson Kemper	1874-1878
Edmund Randolph	1786-1788	Frederick W. M. Holliday	1878-1882
Beverly Randolph	1788-1791	William Evelyn Cameron	1882-1886
Henry Lee	1791-1794	Fitzhugh Lee	1886-1890
Robert Brooke	1794-1796	Philip Watkins McKinley	1890-1894
James Wood	1796-1799	Charles Triplett O'Ferrall	1894-1898
Hardin Burnley	1799	James Hoge Tyler	1898-1902
John Pendleton	1799	Andrew Jackson Montague	1902-1906
James Monroe	1799-1802	Claude Augustus Swanson	1906-1910
John Page	1802-1805	William Hodges Mann	1910-1914
William Cabell	1805-1808	Henry Carter Stuart	1914-1918
John Tyler, Sr.	1808-1811	Westmoreland Davis	1918-1922
James Monroe	1811	Elbert Lee Trinkle	1922-1926
George William Smith	1811	Harry Flood Byrd, Sr.	1926-1930
Peyton Randolph	1811-1812	John Garland Pollard	1930-1934
James Barbour	1812-1814	George Campbell Peery	1934-1938
Wilson Cary Nicholas	1814-1816	James Hubert Price	1938-1942
James Patton Preston	1816-1819	Colgate W. Darden, Jr.	1942-1946
Thomas Mann Randolph	1819-1822	William Munford Tuck	1946-1950
James Pleasants	1822-1825	John Steward Battle	1950-1954
John Tyler, Jr.	1825-1827	Thomas B. Stanley	1954-1958
William Branch Giles	1827-1830	James Lindsay Almond, Jr.	1958-1962
John Floyd	1830-1834	Albertis Sydney Harrison, Jr.	1962-1966
Littleton Waller Tazewell	1834-1836	Mills Edwin Godwin, Jr.	1966-1970
Wyndham Robertson	1836-1837	Abner Linwood Holton, Jr.	1970-1974
David Campbell	1837-1840	Mills Edwin Godwin, Jr.	1974-1978
Thomas Walker Gilmer	1840-1841	John Nichols Dalton	1978-1982
John Mercer Patton	1841	Charles Spittal Robb	1982-1986
John Rutherford	1841-1842	Gerald L. Baliles	1986-1990
John Munford Gregory	1842-1843	L. Douglas Wilder	1990-
James McDowell	1843-1846		
William Smith	1846-1849		
John Buchanan Floyd	1849-1852		
Joseph Johnson	1852-1856		

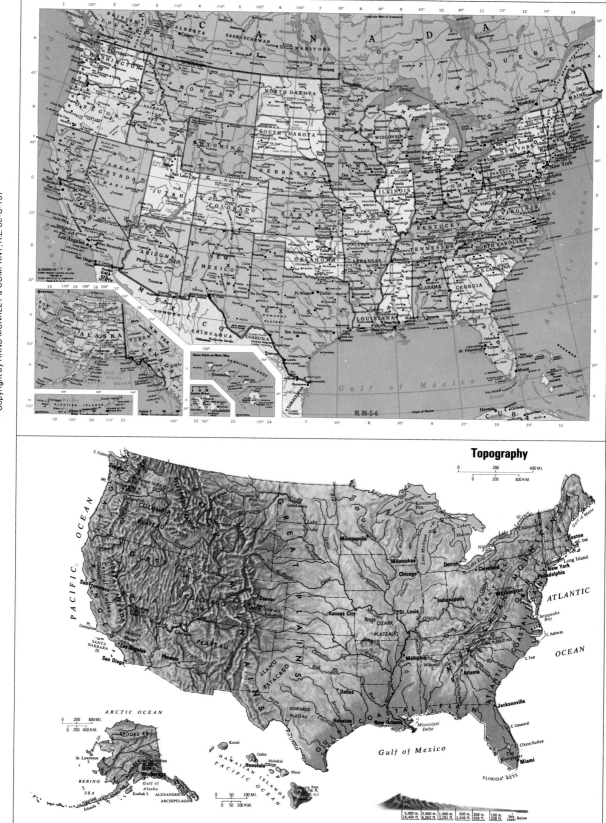

Topography

MAP KEY

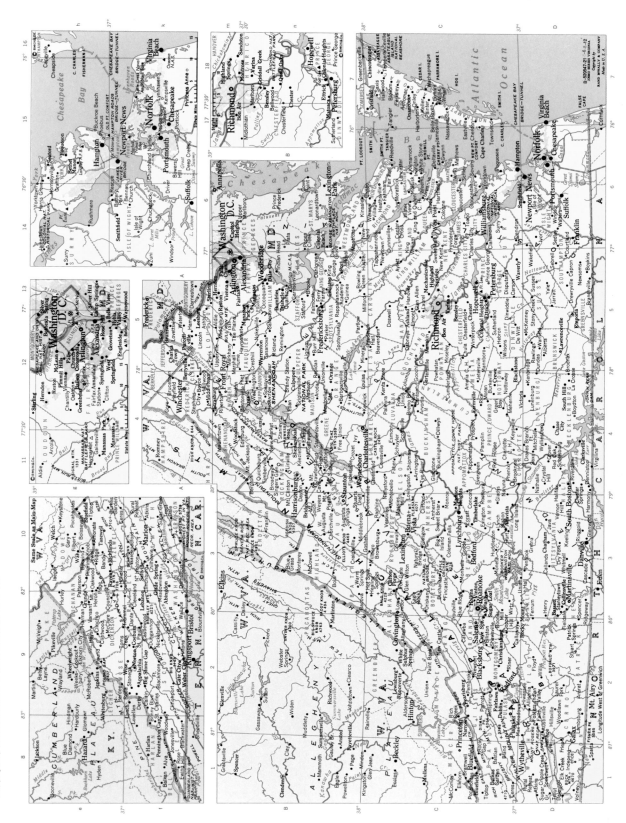

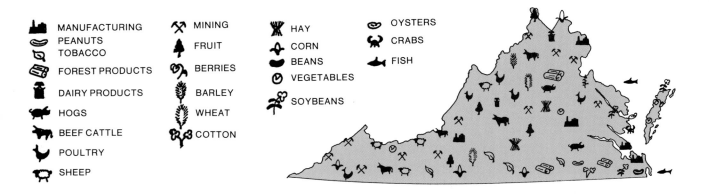

MANUFACTURING
PEANUTS
TOBACCO
FOREST PRODUCTS
DAIRY PRODUCTS
HOGS
BEEF CATTLE
POULTRY
SHEEP

MINING
FRUIT
BERRIES
BARLEY
WHEAT
COTTON

HAY
CORN
BEANS
VEGETABLES
SOYBEANS

OYSTERS
CRABS
FISH

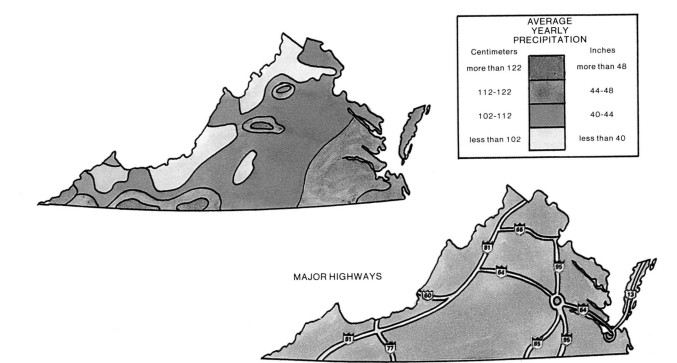

AVERAGE
YEARLY
PRECIPITATION

Centimeters		Inches
more than 122		more than 48
112-122		44-48
102-112		40-44
less than 102		less than 40

MAJOR HIGHWAYS

POPULATION
DENSITY

Number of persons per square kilometer		Number of persons per square mile
more than 100		more than 250
40 to 100		100 to 250
20 to 40		50 to 100
Less than 20		Less than 50

TOPOGRAPHY

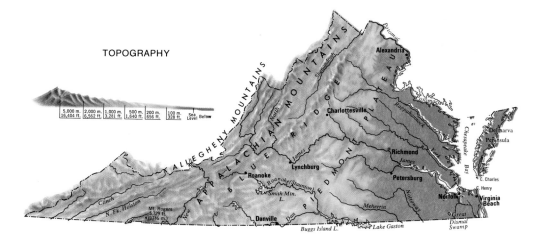

Courtesy of Hammond, Incorporated
Maplewood, New Jersey

COUNTIES

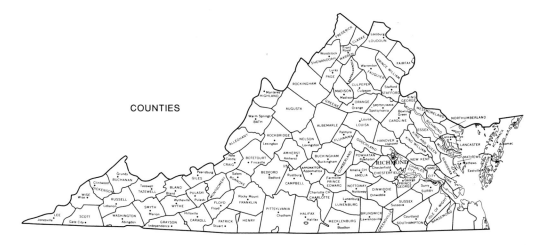

Shenandoah Caverns are among the most colorful of the many scenic caves in the Shenandoah Valley region.

INDEX

Page numbers that appear in boldface type indicate illustrations

138

Each May, nine hundred men from Virginia Military Institute (VMI) gather at New Market Battlefield Park to reenact the Civil War battle that took place there.

Picture Identifications

Front Cover: Cumberland Gap
Back Cover: Dogwood in bloom at Monticello
Pages 2-3: Naked River Overlook, Blue Ridge Mountains
Page 6: The Governor's Palace, Williamsburg
Pages 8-9: Autumn in Shenandoah National Park
Page 18: Montage of Virginians
Page 22: Full-sized replicas of the *Susan Constant,* the *Godspeed,* and the *Discovery,* the ships
that brought the first settlers to Jamestown
Page 36: Statue of George Washington in the Great Hall of the George Washington Masonic
National Memorial in Alexandria
Pages 42-43: *Storming of a Redoubt at Yorktown,* by Eugene Lami, 1840
Pages 52-53: Virginians in Confederate uniforms participate in a Civil War reenactment
Page 62: Woman welding bomb casings in an American munitions factory during World War I
Page 73: The Capitol, Richmond
Pages 82-83: A Williamsburg scene
Pages 90-91: A covered bridge in the Shenandoah Valley
Page 108: Montage showing the state flag, the state bird (cardinal), the state tree (flowering
dogwood), the state animal (foxhound), and the state flower (flowering dogwood)

About the Author

Sylvia McNair is the author of numerous books for adults and young
people about interesting places. A graduate of Oberlin College, she has
toured all fifty of the United States and more than thirty foreign countries.
Her travels have included many visits to all sections of Virginia. Always
interested in education, she served for six years on a district school board in
Illinois. McNair now lives in Evanston, Illinois. She has three sons, one
daughter, and two grandsons.

Picture Acknowledgments

H. Armstrong Roberts: © G. Ahrens: Front cover
Third Coast Stock Source: © Ken Dequaine: Back cover; © Steve Solum: Pages 2-3, 5, 15 (left), 33 (top left), 41, 70 (right)
Folio, Inc.: © Art Stein: Page 4
Tom Stack & Associates: © Tom Algire Photography: Page 6
Root Resources: © James Blank: Pages 8-9, 21 (right), 99, 101, 103 (right); © Bill Thomas: Pages 12, 78 (left), 88 (right); © Anthony Mercieca: Page 13 (left); © J.D. Images: Pages 52-53; © Barry Fitzgerald: Pages 89, 118; © Ruth Chin: Page 103 (left)
Shostal Associates: Pages 18 (middle right), 25, 46 (right), 47, 61 (left), 93, 94, 104, 105 (left), 138; © Bryan Allen: Pages 11, 95; © Anthony Mercieca: Page 13 (top right); © Eric Carle: Page 22; © David Forbert: Pages 73, 102; © Bob Glander: Page 77; © L. Miller: Page 105 (right); © Gene Ahrens: Page 121
Photri: Pages 18 (bottom left), 24 (right), 39 (left), 50, 66 (right), 96, 108 (top left and tree), 115 (left); © Neil L. Shipley: Page 13 (bottom right); © Eugene L. Drifmeyer: Pages 15 (right), 141; © Nick Sebastian: Page 21 (left); © John R. McCauley: Pages 33 (bottom left), 82-83, 88 (left); © B. Kulik: Page 98, 115 (right); © Lani N. Howe: Page 108 (bottom right)
© **Jerry Hennen:** Page 17
© **Mary Ann Brockman:** Pages 18 (top left), 24 (left), 29 (right), 66 (left)
Focus/Virginia: © James Kirby: Page 18 (top right); © J.C. Mantilla: Page 18 (bottom right)
© **Arch McLean:** Page 26
Historical Pictures Service, Inc., Chicago: Pages 29 (left), 49, 57 (left), 128 (Jones and Lee), 129 (bottom), 130 (McGuffey and Reed), 131 (top)
The Granger Collection: Pages 30, 31, 35, 46 (left), 56, 60 (top, middle, bottom left), 62, 64, 65 (both pictures)
© **James P. Rowan:** Page 33 (top right)
© **SuperStock International:** Pages 36, 78 (right), 79, 85, 90-91, 97, 111, 112
Cameramann International Ltd.: Pages 39 (right), 61 (right), 76 (right)
Virginia State Library and Archives: Pages 42-43, 45
The National Park Service: Page 57 (right)
The Bettmann Archive: Pages 60 (bottom right), 126 (bottom), 128 (Jackson), 130 (bottom)
UPI/Bettmann Newsphotos: Pages 69, 126 (top), 127 (Fitzgerald), 129 (top)
AP/Wide World Photos, Inc.: Pages 70 (left), 127 (top and bottom), 129 (Marshall), 130 (Poe)
© **Joan Dunlop:** Pages 76 (left), 86
© **Martin Hintz:** Page 81
© **Kirkendall/Spring:** Page 107
Odyssey Productions: © Charlene Wrobel: Page 108 (bottom left)
Library of Congress: Pages 127 (Clark), 131 (Wilson)
U.S. Bureau of Printing and Engraving: Pages 128 (top), 129 (Madison), 131 (Taylor)
Tuskegee Institute: Page 131 (Washington)
Len W. Meents: Maps on pages 93, 98, 101, 102, 104, 107, 136
Courtesy Flag Research Center, Winchester, Massachusetts 01890: Flag on page 108